Ethics and Religion

Ethics and Religion explores philosophical issues that link the two areas. Many people question whether God is the source of morality. Divine command theory says that God's will creates the moral order, therefore ethical truths are true because of God's will. Natural law, in contrast, accepts ethical truths that do not depend on God's will but perhaps depend on his reason or creation. The book develops strong and defensible versions of both views and provides strong new versions of the divine command theory and the natural law theory. It also deals with ethics and atheism: how atheists object on ethical grounds to belief in God and how they view ethics. Gensler defends belief in God from their objections. *Ethics and Religion* further analyzes related concepts, such as practical reason, the golden rule, ethics and evolution, the problem of evil, and the fine-tuning argument.

Harry J. Gensler, S.J., is Professor of Philosophy at Loyola University Chicago. His thirteen books include *Ethics and the Golden Rule* (2013), *Ethics: A Contemporary Introduction* (2011), *Introduction to Logic* (2010), and *Anthology of Catholic Philosophy* (2005). A fanatical outdoorsperson, he has bicycled from Los Angeles to New York and has hiked from Georgia to Maine and from Mexico to Canada. His website, www.harryhiker.com, has more information on him.

Cambridge Studies in Religion, Philosophy, and Society

Series Editors

PAUL MOSER, *Loyola University Chicago*
CHAD MEISTER, *Bethel College*

This is a series of interdisciplinary texts devoted to major-level courses in religion, philosophy, and related fields. It includes original, current, and wide-spanning contributions by leading scholars from various disciplines that (a) focus on the central academic topics in religion and philosophy, (b) are seminal and up to date regarding recent developments in scholarship on the various key topics, and (c) incorporate, with needed precision and depth, the major differing perspectives and backgrounds – the central voices on the major religions and the religious, philosophical, and sociological viewpoints that cover the intellectual landscape today. Cambridge Studies in Religion, Philosophy, and Society is a direct response to this recent and widespread interest and need.

Recent Books in the Series
Roger Trigg, *Religious Diversity: Philosophical and Political Dimensions*
John Cottingham, *Philosophy of Religion: Towards a More Humane Approach*
William J. Wainwright, *Reason, Revelation, and Devotion: Inference and Argument in Religion*

Ethics and Religion

HARRY J. GENSLER

Loyola University Chicago

CAMBRIDGE
UNIVERSITY PRESS

32 Avenue of the Americas, New York, NY 10013-2473, USA

Cambridge University Press is part of the University of Cambridge.

It furthers the University's mission by disseminating knowledge in the pursuit of education, learning, and research at the highest international levels of excellence.

www.cambridge.org
Information on this title: www.cambridge.org/9781107647169

© Harry J. Gensler 2016

First published 2016

Printed in the United States of America by Sheridan Books, Inc

A catalog record for this publication is available from the British Library.

Library of Congress Cataloging in Publication Data
Names: Gensler, Harry J., 1945– author.
Title: Ethics and religion / Harry J. Gensler, Loyola University Chicago.
Description: New York : Cambridge University Press, 2016. | Series: Cambridge studies in religion, philosophy, and society | Includes bibliographical references and index.
Identifiers: LCCN 2015042176 | ISBN 9781107052444
Subjects: LCSH: Religion and ethics. | Religious ethics. | Natural law.
Classification: LCC BJ47 .G46 2016 | DDC 205–dc23
LC record available at http://lccn.loc.gov/2015042176

ISBN 978-1-107-05244-4 Hardback
ISBN 978-1-107-64716-9 Paperback

Contents

Preface

Ethics and Religion explores some of the major philosophical issues that link these two important areas of life. For many people, the burning issue is whether God is the source of morality and whether ethics is possible without religion. There are two traditional views here, with many variations. *Divine command theory* says that God's will creates the moral order (so ethical truths are true because of God's will), whereas *natural law* accepts ethical truths that don't depend on God's will (but perhaps depend on his reason or on his creation). Although I favor natural law, I try to develop strong and defensible versions of both views. With both views, I'll try to show how belief in God can deepen ethics – as it can deepen every area of life.

I also deal with ethics and atheism: how atheists object on ethical grounds to belief in God and how they view ethics; I'll also respond to their objections.

I hit many related topics, such as how to develop divine command theory (e.g., through semantic definitions or property identity); how we can know God's will; how to understand God's wisdom, love, and goodness; how to develop natural law (including practical reason and the golden rule); how evolution and science relate to ethics and religion; what difference belief in God makes to ethics; what duties we have toward those of other perspectives on faith; whether militant atheists make a good case against religion; atheistic religion; the problem of evil; and the fine-tuning argument.

Is there anything new to say about *ethics and religion*? I think so. There's been much activity on this during the last few years, and my book argues for some innovative ideas.

This book is part of the Cambridge Studies in Religion, Philosophy, and Society series, so the book is simply written, assumes little previous knowledge, and should be accessible to advanced undergraduates. But the book is also deep enough for graduate students, seminarians, other ministry students, teachers, and experts in the area. It could be used in various courses, including ones in philosophy of religion, moral philosophy, and moral theology. The clear style should make it accessible to sophisticated general readers. There's much interest in ethics and religion these days, and I hope that this book will fill a need.

I thank Marquette University (where I held the Wade Chair in Spring 2014, which gave me much time to write), Kyle Whitaker (my teaching assistant there, who read early chapters and made suggestions), and Tom Carson (my colleague in the Loyola Chicago philosophy department, who read the whole manuscript and made suggestions).

I

Introduction

Ethics and religion are large and important areas of life. This book explores some of the main philosophical issues linking the two. To show where we're going, I'll first clarify three key ideas: philosophy, ethics, and religion.

1.1 Philosophy

We can explore how ethics and religion connect using various disciplines: history, law, anthropology, sociology, literature, biology, philosophy, and so forth. Our philosophical approach rationally debates big questions about ethics and religion. *Philosophy is reasoning about the big questions of life.*

If you search the Web for "ethics and religion," the biggest issue is this (with many people arguing yes or no): "Is God the source of morality (so without God we can't have genuine duties)?" This will be a central issue here. This isn't the same issue as "Can atheists have a morality and be good people?" Practically all thinkers answer yes to this. Our issue, rather, is whether morality makes sense without God.

Religious philosophers tend, roughly, to be of two camps. Some see ethics as God's commands (Part I, Chapters 2 and 3), while others see ethics as natural laws that have some independence from God's will (Part II, Chapters 4–6). Both views have evolved sophisticated forms. I'll argue that the best view for religious thinkers is a combination I call *divine-preference natural law*.

Along the way, we'll get into other issues, such as, "How can we know right from wrong?" "How does morality relate to evolution?" "What

does loving-our-neighbor mean?" "How does the golden rule work?"
"How are the commandments against stealing, lying, killing, and adultery
best understood and defended?" "What duties do we have toward those
of other faith perspectives?" "What are our duties toward God?" and
"What difference does belief in God make to ethics?"

Part III, on ethics and atheism (Chapters 7 and 8), studies how atheists
object on ethical grounds to belief in God and how they view ethics. I'll
also respond to their objections.

Philosophy differs from theology. Traditionally and roughly, *philosophy* uses only human reason, while *theology* adds divine revelation[1]
(perhaps from the Bible or church teaching). We'll mostly stay on the
philosophy side of the divide, but sometimes (as in §1.3) we'll wander
across the fuzzy border.

1.2 Ethics

My opening sentence called ethics an "area of life," but we can also see
ethics as *moral philosophy*: the *philosophical study* of this area. Moral
philosophy focuses on two key questions:

1. *Metaethics*: What is the nature of morality, and how can we reason
   about moral issues?
2. *Normative ethics*: How ought we to live?

Moral philosophy, accordingly, has two main branches.[2]

Metaethics studies the nature and methodology of morality. It asks
questions such as, "What do 'good' and 'ought' mean?" "What are goodness and obligation?" "Do moral judgments express cultural conventions,
personal feelings, self-evident truths, or divine commands?" "Are there
objective moral truths (or facts) about right and wrong?" "How can we
justify, rationally defend, or reason about moral beliefs, if we can?"

Normative ethics studies how we ought to live; it proposes general or
specific norms, values, and virtues. It asks questions such as, "What are
the basic principles of right and wrong?" "What is good or worthwhile
in life?" "What is a just society like?" "What makes someone a good

---

[1] See St. Thomas Aquinas's (1274) *Summa Theologica* (I, q. 1, a. 1).
[2] See my ethics textbook (Gensler 2011a), anthology (Gensler, Spurgin, and Swindal 2004),
and encyclopedia (Gensler and Spurgin 2008).

person?" "What are the basic virtues and vices?" "What are the basic human rights?" "Is killing ever justified?" "Is abortion right or wrong?" This book deals with both areas. Our initial question ("Is God the source of morality?") is about metaethics. I'll use *ethics* and *morality* interchangeably.

1.3 Religion

Occasionally this book takes *religion* in a wide sense, to include monotheistic, polytheistic, and nontheistic religions. I use this wide sense in Section 6.6, when I say that the golden rule is common to practically every religion, and in Section 7.4, when I discuss atheistic religions such as Humanistic Judaism.

I usually take *"religion"* more narrowly, as "monotheistic religion." My *Ethics and Religion* book is mostly about ethics and God. "God" is understood as in the great monotheistic religions, roughly as Copleston and Russell (1948: 390) agreed to in their radio debate: "a supreme personal being – distinct from the world and creator of the world." While I'm Christian,[3] most of the same issues are important in Judaism, Islam, and other religions with a supreme God.[4]

Religions are often analyzed as *creed-code-cult*, where *code* usually has much moral content. To keep us from thinking too abstractly about God's will, it will be good to look at the moral content of one particular religion. Being Christian, I'll talk about the Bible. Those of another faith might reflect on the moral content of their faith.

The Bible is a faith account of God's action and humanity's response. While the Bible lacks systematic ethical treatises, it teaches morality in its stories, heroes, sermons, prayers, exhortations, proverbs, and commandments.

While the Jewish Law in the Old Testament has 613 precepts, most central are the Ten Commandments (Exodus 20:1–17 and Deuteronomy

---

[3] I'm Catholic (a Jesuit priest) and interested in world religions and interfaith relations. My last book, *Ethics and the Golden Rule* (Gensler 2013), had symbols for eight world religions on the cover and said much about the golden rule in the religions of the world.

[4] Harris (2003) and Brody (1974) talk about divine command theory and its foes in Judaism. Al-Attar (2010) and Michel (2010, 197–99) discuss this dispute in Islam; Al-Attar (2010, 109) asks, Does God *create* or *clarify* morality?

5:6–21). We can divide these into three groups. The first group has duties to God:[5]

1. You shall not worship false gods.
2. You shall not take God's name in vain.
3. Keep holy the Sabbath.

Other duties toward God include faith, hope, and love; obedience; and prayerful responses of praise and thanksgiving. Duties to other people are indirectly duties to God, because they express obedience to him and concern for his creatures.

The second group has duties to family:

4. Honor your father and mother.
6. You shall not commit adultery.
9. You shall not covet your neighbor's spouse.

For a family to flourish, the husband-wife bond must be strong; adultery typically harms or destroys families. Further duties between spouses include affection, communication, and avoiding cruelty. Children are to honor their parents; this involves obedience and, later, friendship with and caring for parents in their old age. Parents are to care for their children and help them grow into responsible adults; later, they're to provide emotional support for their adult children through life's difficulties. There also are duties to brothers and sisters, to other relatives, and to those of one's social units (such as villages and nations).

The third group has duties to everyone:

5. You shall not kill.
7. You shall not steal.
8. You shall not bear false witness.
10. You shall not covet your neighbor's goods.

We are not to kill, steal, lie, or be envious. Other duties are to show respect and politeness toward others, help those in need, show gratitude and reparation, and be just toward the weak and powerless (as emphasized by the prophets).

Wisdom and love are key. So we have Nathan's similar-situation story that helps King David see his error (2 Samuel 12:1–13), commandments to

---

[5] Traditions differ on how to number the commandments and on which books constitute the Bible. In giving passages from sacred texts, I use my own words to express the ideas clearly in modern American English.

love God above all things and one's neighbor as oneself (Deuteronomy 6:5 and Leviticus 19:18), and the golden rule (Tobit 4:15) and its application to aliens ("Don't oppress aliens; you know how it feels to be an alien from when you were aliens yourself in Egypt"; Exodus 23:9). There's some universalism from the beginning, as Genesis 1:27 tells of *all* humans being created in God's image and likeness.

The Old Testament was an agreement between God and the Jews: God would guide and protect them, and they'd worship and obey God. The New Testament extends this to all.

In the New Testament, the most important commandments are the love norms and the golden rule:

- Love the Lord your God with all your heart and soul and strength. This is the greatest commandment. The second is similar: Love your neighbor as yourself. These sum up the Law and the prophets. (Matthew 22:36–40)
- Treat others as you want to be treated, for this sums up the Law and the prophets. (Matthew 7:12)

Also important are the beatitudes (such as "Blessed are those who suffer persecution for the sake of doing right, for theirs is the kingdom of heaven"; Matthew 5:3–10), loving your enemies (Matthew 5:38–48), the Good Samaritan parable that illustrates this (Luke 10:29–37), Jesus's example ("As I have loved you, so you are to love one another; this is how people will know you are my disciples"; John 13:34–35), Paul's poem about love ("Love is patient and kind, not jealous or pompous"; 1 Corinthians 13:1–13), and Paul about how nonbelievers can know the moral law ("The demands of the law are written on their hearts"; Romans 2:13–15).

The Bible gradually develops toward higher approaches to morality. It can appeal to higher motives (unselfish love and gratitude to God) or lower motives (punishments and rewards); this is fitting, because it has to appeal to many people.

The Bible and sacred texts of other religions don't explicitly discuss most of the issues that this present book deals with – such as "Is God the source of morality?" So any scriptural contribution to these issues would have to be indirect.

PART I

ETHICS AS GOD'S COMMANDS

2

Divine Command Theory

Is God the source of morality, so without God, we couldn't have genuine duties? This is a burning issue for philosophers and nonphilosophers alike. Politicians, preachers, and parents often insist that the very existence of society requires the strong moral values that only religion and religious moral education can provide. Atheists protest that they're misunderstood and discriminated against and can be as moral as believers.

This chapter considers the traditional *divine command theory* (DCT), which sees genuine duties as depending on God's will; I'll introduce DCT using C. S. Lewis's somewhat similar view. Chapter 3 discusses modified DCTs that assert a qualified dependence of morality on God's will.

2.1 C. S. Lewis

Clive Staples Lewis (1898–1963) was born in Belfast. He taught medieval and Renaissance literature for thirty years at Oxford and then ten more at Cambridge. He became famous for his children's books and Christian apologetics. His books sold 100 million copies and remain influential today; a show of hands in my logic course, with mostly philosophy graduate students, showed that most had read Lewis.

Lewis became an atheist as a teenager, driven by the problem of evil: "My argument against God was that the universe seemed so cruel and unjust" (Lewis 1952: 38). In midlife, he returned to God as an Anglican and came to defend "mere Christianity" (what Christian groups hold in common).

The BBC asked him to do radio talks about his faith. Lewis accepted, even though he saw himself as an amateur and beginner in religion; he thought that, as a layman and former atheist, he might have something special to say to people who struggle with faith. His classic apologetic work, *Mere Christianity* (Lewis 1952), came from earlier radio talks and sold 11 million copies. We'll focus on his "Right and Wrong: A Clue to the Meaning of the Universe."

Lewis provides an ideal introduction for us because he's clear, insightful, entertaining, and influential – and avoids technical issues better discussed later.

Lewis (1952: 3–32) argues that there's an objective moral law and that this requires the existence of God.

First, Lewis contends that pretty much everyone recognizes objective moral duties. He defends this in various ways.

We've all heard quarreling. People say things like, "How'd you like it if someone did the same to you?" – "That's my seat, I was there first" – "Leave him alone, he isn't harming you" – "Give me some of your orange, I gave you some of mine" – "But you promised." People here appeal, not to likes and dislikes, but to standards that they expect others to recognize. These others typically accept the standard but claim that their action doesn't violate it or that they have a good excuse for violating it. So both parties recognize a law or rule of fair play or decent behavior. We assume that everyone knows the standards (except perhaps an unusual defective individual).

But don't different cultures disagree deeply about morality? There are moral differences, yes, but not a total difference. Moralities are mostly the same. People differ on what people you ought to be unselfish to – whether only your family, or your fellow countrymen, or everyone. But they agree that you ought not to just put yourself first. People differ on whether you should have one wife or four. But they agree that you must not simply have any woman you like. The golden rule ("Do as you would be done by") sums up what everyone has always known to be right (Lewis 1952: 82).

People who say that they don't believe in a real Right and Wrong will go back on this later. They may break their promise to you, but if you try breaking one to them they'll complain "it's not fair." A nation may say treaties don't matter; but then they spoil their case by saying that the treaty they want to break was unfair. But if there's no Right and Wrong, then what's the difference between a fair treaty and an unfair one?

Some object that the so-called moral law is just a social convention put into us by education. But we may be educated about objective truths, like arithmetic additions. And social conventions (like which side of the road to drive on) vary widely, while basic moral norms don't. We all think some moralities are higher than others (loving your neighbor being higher than Nazi genocide) – which presupposes that some moralities more closely conform to what is really Right or Wrong.

Some object that the English used to persecute witches: did that accord with an objective moral rule? But here there's a difference, not about moral principle, but about facts. People back then thought there were witches with power from the devil to kill their neighbors. Today we reject such beliefs. There need be no difference in moral principle here: the difference is simply about matters of fact.

Some object that norms of right and wrong just describe how people act. But that isn't true – since we often act *against* moral norms that we recognize. These norms are something we don't always follow and yet know we ought to follow.

But how do objective duties lead to God?

Since the beginning, Lewis claims, people have been wondering how the universe came to be. Very roughly, there are two views. The *materialist view* says that matter always existed, nobody knows why, and matter has, by a fluke, produced thinking beings like us. Recent forms of this talk about evolution and the huge number of planets; it's likely that at least one planet would evolve intelligent life. In contrast, the *religious view* says that behind the universe there exists a great mind – with consciousness, purposes, and preferences – who created the universe in part to produce intelligent beings like us. Both views emerge wherever there are thinking people.[1]

Science cannot decide between the views. Science is about observables and correlating observations. It can't tell us why there's a universe or what deeper meaning it may have.

Fortunately, we have inside information. As humans, we find that we're subject to a moral law that we didn't create. If there were a controlling power outside the universe, it couldn't show itself to us as an observable fact inside the universe; it could only show itself *inside ourselves*, as an influence or command. And that's what we find. So we get to a Something directing the universe that appears in us as a law urging us to do right

[1] McGowan (2013: 63–167) sketches the history of atheism from the ancient world (including India, China, Greece, and Israel) to the twenty-first century.

and making us uncomfortable when we do wrong. We have to assume it's more like a mind than anything else we know; the only other thing we know is matter, which can't give instructions. And so, through our knowledge of right and wrong, we come to God (in the vague sense of *a mind-like source of the moral law* – Christian revelation gives a fuller story).

Lewis's approach allows atheists (as he was earlier in life) to know right from wrong; it sees basic moral norms as built into us and thus known to virtually everyone. It allows atheists to be good people, even though they don't see that morality presupposes belief in God. And it answers his objection to God, on the basis of the universe being so unjust; this objection presupposes an objective moral distinction between just and unjust – and so commits us to believing in God (Lewis 1952: 38).

Lewis's reasoning goes like this

> There's an objective moral law.
> If there's an objective moral law, then there's a God.
> ∴ There's a God.

Lewis defended premise 1, although some may still disagree. But he said little about premise 2: "*If there's an objective moral law, then there's a God.*" Why believe this? G. E. Moore, who also taught at Cambridge, accepted an objective moral law but rejected God. What would Lewis say to Moore?

Morality might depend on God in at least three ways:

- *Source of duties*: Only God can make acts right or wrong.
- *Moral motivation*: Only those who believe in God can have adequate motivation to live morally.
- *Moral knowledge*: Only those who believe in God can know right from wrong.

The first option best fits Lewis and is the most plausible. So I propose this reconstruction of his argument:

> There's an objective moral law.
> If there's an objective moral law, then there's a source of the moral law.
> If there's a source of the moral law, then there's a God.
> ∴ There's a God.

We need to consider premises 2 and 3.

Premise 3: "*If there's a source of the moral law, then there's a God.*" One might defend this by arguing that this source could only be a nonperson, or you, or other individuals, or society, or God. But the nonreligious alternatives won't work. The source of obligation can't be

- a nonperson – since these are inferior to persons and thus can't impose obligations on persons
- you (the agent) – since then you wouldn't have binding obligations, since you could release yourself at will
- other individuals or society – since these have no moral authority over us if they tell us to do wrong

God is the only workable source of an objective moral law. So believing in this moral law commits us to believing in God.

But this goes much too fast. Some see morality as objective but having a source other than God, for example,

- *Ideal observer*: Moral norms express how we'd want people to live if we were fully rational (informed, consistent, impartial, and so on).
- *Social contract*: Moral norms are conventions that rational individuals would agree to for their mutual advantage.

These need to be considered.

Premise 2: *"If there's an objective moral law, then there's a source of the moral law."* Believers like Socrates and agnostics like G. E. Moore would deny this. They see moral ideas like "Hating people is evil" as necessary truths that need no source. What's the *source* of "$x = x$" or "$2 + 2 = 4$"? Who or what made these true? These are true of their very nature; they aren't true because something made them true. Basic moral truths may be similar. Perhaps "Hating people is evil" is an independent, objective moral truth; it's true in itself instead of being true because something made it true. This is the *independent-duties view*.

So perhaps objective duties can be based on nonreligious ideas like *independent duties*, *ideal observers*, or *social contracts*; it would be a large task to show that these can't work. And some question whether *God's will* (which could have been arbitrary or cruel) gives an adequate basis for objective duties. So Lewis's reasoning doesn't give a strong argument for God's existence.[2]

---

[2] Or we might claim that *every law requires a lawgiver* and *only God could give the moral law*; Anscombe (1958) hints at this. But many laws (like ones in logic and mathematics) seem not to require a lawgiver; so it's doubtful that *every law* requires a lawgiver. Or maybe *every moral law* requires a lawgiver? But then it's less clear that moral norms should be considered "laws."

2.2 DCT

Thinkers who believe that God is the source of morality often endorse
divine command theory (also called *DCT* or *theological voluntarism*).
DCT says that actions are good or bad, right or wrong, *because* of God's
will (his desires or commands).[3] God's will creates the moral order and
the right/wrong distinction.

Lewis seems to hold this, but he doesn't express himself that way. He
mainly argues for the existence of God. Most DCT thinkers, however,
don't appeal to ethics to try to establish the existence of God; instead,
they appeal to a prior belief in God to argue that ethics depends on God's
will.

DCT bases morality on *God's will*. But there are at least four ways
that God might be the source of morality. God might make acts good or
bad through

- *His will*: Kindness is good because God desires kindness.
- *His nature*: Kindness is good because God is kind.[4]
- *His creation*: Kindness is good for us because God created us with
  a certain nature, and practical reason can discover that it's good for
  beings of this nature to be kind.
- *His mind*: Kindness is good because God (through direct insight or
  practical reason) knows that kindness is good.

The rest of this chapter discusses objections to the first option (DCT); the
next chapter considers modified DCTs designed to avoid objections. Still
later, we'll consider the "creation" and "mind" options, which are part
of the rival natural law view.

2.3 Euthyphro and Evil Actions

Socrates, a philosopher of ancient Greece, was a religious person who
tried to follow the divine will. He saw ethics as closely connected with
religion. But the *Euthyphro* dialogue pictures him as rejecting DCT,

---

[3] Until §3.5, in discussing DCT, I'll be loose about whether to say "good" / "bad" or
"right" / "wrong," and whether to say "desires" or "commands."

[4] Here we ought to imitate God's *nature*: "Be like God." But be like God *in what ways*?
Are we to create a world? Perhaps we ought imitate God in ways that God *wants* us to be
imitate him; but this brings us back to DCT. Zagzebski (2004) may avoid these objections;
we imitate God's motives and follow what Christ would do in a similar situation.

largely on the basis of a penetrating question. I'll express his question in my own words.[5]

Suppose that God desires all good actions. We can ask:

> Is a good action good because God desires it?
> Or does God desire it because it's good?

Assume that kindness is good and God desires it. Which is based on which? Is kindness good because God desires it? Or does God desire kindness because it's already good?

Socrates and most people would take the second alternative. God desires kindness because he knows that it's good. His desires don't make it good. Instead, he wouldn't desire it if it weren't already good. But then kindness is good prior to and independently of God's will. It would presumably be good even if there were no God. This alternative rejects DCT.

Socrates held the *independent-duties view*. Basic moral norms (like "Kindness is good" and "Hatred is bad") are necessary truths: like "2 + 2 = 4," they're true of their very nature and not true because someone or something made them true. God knows these truths and his will follows them; but he didn't make them true any more than he made "2 + 2 = 4" true.

DCT must take the first alternative: kindness is good because God desires it.[6] Kindness then wouldn't be good if God didn't desire it. Prior to God's desires, kindness is neither good nor bad. This answer, while possible, seems implausible and seems to make ethics arbitrary.

Or assume that hatred is bad and God forbids it. Is hatred bad because God forbids it (so if he didn't forbid it, then it wouldn't be bad)? Or does God forbid it because it's already bad? This second alternative seems more plausible but requires giving up DCT.

The related *evil-actions objection* goes as follows:

> If actions are good just because God desires them, then *continually hating others* would be good if God desired it.
> *Continually hating others* wouldn't be good if God desired it.
> ∴ Actions aren't good just because God desires them.

---

[5] Lane Cooper's translation of Socrates's question (*Euthyphro* 10a) goes "Is what is holy holy because the gods approve it, or do they approve it because it is holy?" (Idziak 1979: 41). I'll consider a monotheistic version.

[6] Some take this alternative. Gabriel Biel (1425–95) wrote: "It is not because something is good or just, that God wills it; but because God wills it, it is therefore good and just" (72). Others who said similar things include Pierre D'Ailly (64), Jean Gerson (66), Martin Luther (95), John Calvin (101), and several Puritan thinkers (104–5). These page numbers are for Idziak (1979).

We often criticize ethical theories that could prescribe evil actions. To one who claims that "good" means "socially accepted," we ask, "If hating others were socially accepted, would that make it good?" To one who claims that "good" means "what I like," we ask, "If you were to like hating others, would that make it good?" Likewise, to DCT, we can ask, "If God were to desire hatred, would that make it good?" We can repeat the question using *any evil action*, which would become good if God desired it. So DCT, far from making ethics objective, makes it arbitrary.[7]

DCT can respond in two ways. William of Ockham (1287–1347) would deny premise 2 and say that, yes, anything God desired, even continual hatred, would become good (Idziak 1979: 55–57). This sounds extreme, even if we add that God is unlikely to command such things; but it's a possible response.

Many DCT supporters respond that God *can't* command evil things, since he's *good* by nature. But what does it mean here to call God and his actions "good"? I give you three choices:

1. *What God does accords with his desires.* DCT has to accept this. But then "God's actions are good" reduces to "God does what he desires," and so is trivialized (since even hateful people can do what they desire).[8]
2. *What God does accords with standards of goodness that hold independently of his will.* This rejects DCT.
3. *What God does is loving.* But then why can't *our* actions be good because they're loving? Here again, we'd have a standard of goodness other than God's desires – which is incompatible with DCT.

So all three options bring problems. Chapter 3 will consider modified DCTs designed to overcome these problems.

---

7   Ralph Cudworth (1617–88) objected: "Whence it follows unavoidably, that nothing can be imagined so grossly wicked, or so foully unjust or dishonest, but if it were supposed to be commanded by this omnipotent deity, must . . . become holy, just and righteous" (Idziak 1979: 158).

8   The third Earl of Shaftesbury (1671–1713) objected: "If the mere will, decree, or law of God be said absolutely to constitute right and wrong, then are these latter words [about God's justice and goodness] of no significancy at all." Francis Hutcheson (1694–1746) likewise said: "But to call the laws of the supreme Deity *good*, or *holy*, or *just*, if all goodness, holiness, and justice be constituted by [these] *laws*, . . . must be an insignificant tautology, amounting to no more than this, 'that God *wills* what he *wills*'" (Idziak 1979: 198–99).

2.4 Sovereignty and the Bible

The *sovereignty argument* bases DCT on God's absolute sovereignty over all of reality, and thus over every law and fact:

All laws and facts of *every* sort depend on God's will.
∴ All *moral* laws and facts depend on God's will.

Duties independent of God would objectionably detract from God's sovereign and omnipotent rule over all reality.[9]

However, there seem to be laws and facts that are beyond God's control and that he cannot change, for example,

- basic logical laws (like the law of noncontradiction)
- $x = x$
- $2 + 2 \neq 87$
- the fact that God isn't stupid
- the fact that God exists

It's strange to think God could have made these all false – that he could have brought it about that contradictions are simultaneously true, that $x \neq x$, that $2 + 2 = 87$, that he's stupid, and that he never existed. Does it really detract from God's greatness if he can't bring these about – or can't bring it about that hating others is our highest virtue? We don't mention such abilities when we talk about God's supreme greatness.[10]

Some atheists contend that both answers to the *Euthyphro* question discredit belief in God. Making good *depend* on God leads to absurdity (by the evil-actions argument) while making good *not depend* on God detracts from God's sovereignty. However, I find the sovereignty part questionable.

The *biblical argument* bases DCT on the Bible:

The Bible teaches that good actions are good because God desires them.
Everything that the Bible teaches is true.
∴ Good actions are good because God desires them.

---

[9] Carl Henry (1913–2003) criticized accepting an independent good: "They viewed the good as something to which God was bound rather than as something legislated by him. This prepared the way for an objectionable doctrine of the 'good in itself.' The good then is superior to God" (Idziak 1979: 143).

[10] Richard Price (1723–91) adds: "If for this reason, we must give up the unalterable natures of right and wrong, and make them dependent on the Divine will; we must, for the same reason, give up all necessary truth, and assert the possibility of contradictions" (Idziak 1979: 211).

The Bible uses "good" as interchangeable with "what God desires." God's writing the Ten Commandments on stone tablets teaches DCT (Exodus 20 and Deuteronomy 5), as does Abraham's deciding to sacrifice his son at God's command (Genesis 22).[11] So DCT is the Judeo-Christian view on ethics.[12]

But does the Bible really teach DCT? When I did a theology masters years ago, my professor cautioned against using the Bible to answer questions that the biblical authors didn't ask and wouldn't have immediately understood. By this criterion, it would be illegitimate to use the Bible to establish DCT.

The Bible teaches that *we ought to obey God.* Maybe we ought to obey God because his will reflects a deeper knowledge of duties that hold independently of his will. Then stealing isn't bad because God forbids it; instead, God forbids it because it's already bad. Such non-DCT views are consistent with the Bible.

2.5 Meaning of "Good"

DCT can be *normative* or *semantic*:

- *Normative*: A good action is good because God desires it.
- *Semantic*: "Good action" means "action desired by God."

The semantic DCT entails the normative DCT, but not vice versa; so the normative DCT might be true while yet "good" doesn't mean "desired by God."[13]

The semantic DCT must confront the *circularity problem.* If we define "good" using "God," then we can't define "God" as "the *all-good,*

---

[11] God commands Abraham to kill his son but changes his mind. Does this teach that we must obey God even when this makes no sense to us, because God creates the moral order? Maybe not; Copan (2011: 42–54) and Green (1982) give longer analyses.

[12] Karl Barth, Emil Brunner, Carl Henry, and many other Protestants base DCT on the Bible. Brunner says that the basis for the Good leads us "back to the truth of the Bible, namely, that only that which God wills is good; and thus that we are to will what God wills, because he wills it." Henry criticizes an independent good: "Thereafter, the phrase 'I ought' no longer means 'the sovereign Lord commands.' Rather, it is informed by self-evident truths or by the intuitions of the moral order.... Thus the Christian West enters into a non-Christian orientation" (Idziak 1979: 106–53, 137, 142–43).

[13] William Paley (1743–1805) defined a *right action* as *one that's consistent with God's will* (Idziak 1979: 215–16). Similar definitions may have been implicit in other historical DCT thinkers. The semantic DCT took center stage with the twentieth-century "linguistic turn" in philosophy (see the selections by A. C. Ewing, Kai Nielsen, and Patterson Brown in Idziak 1979); so Robert Adams (1973: 319) saw the traditional DCT as

all-powerful, all-knowing creator of the world." This would make our definitions circular (since we'd use "God" to define "good," and then use "good" to define "God"). The definition would also suggest that there are standards of goodness prior to God's will (instead of God's will creating the standards). So the semantic DCT would do better to define "God" as perhaps "the all-powerful, all-knowing creator of the world," dropping "all-good" from the definition.

This aggravates the evil-actions objection. Suppose the creator desired hatred; would hatred then be good? Surely not! So we can consistently imagine the creator desiring actions that aren't good. But then "good action" doesn't mean "action that the creator desires."[14]

The semantic DCT must deal with the *atheism problem*. Imagine an atheist who says, "Kindness is good, but there's no God." If "X is good" meant "God desires X," then this would be self-contradictory (since it would mean "God desires kindness, but there's no God"). But it isn't self-contradictory. So "X is good" doesn't mean "God desires X." Or we might argue this way:

> If "good" means "desired by God," then atheists can't consistently make positive moral judgments.
> Atheists can consistently make positive moral judgments.[15]
> ∴ "Good" doesn't mean "desired by God."

This argument assumes that atheists aren't contradicting themselves when they make positive moral judgments; but it doesn't assume any positive view about what "good" means.

The semantic DCT might claim that believers and atheists mean different things by "good"; believers mean "desired by God," but atheists mean something else (and so can consistently make positive moral judgments). But then believers and atheists can't really agree or disagree morally. If I say "This is good" (meaning "God desires this") and the atheist says "This is good" (meaning something else), then we agree only verbally. But we can have fruitful moral discussions with people even if we know nothing about their religion; the discussion will mostly go the same way

defining *wrong* as *contrary to God's commands*. More recently, the semantic DCT has tended to be replaced by metaphysical identity claims of the "water = H₂O" sort (§3.7).

[14] The *open-question argument* also has been used against the semantic DCT. If "good" means "what the creator desires," then "This is desired by the creator, but is it good?" would be a self-answering, trivial question, like "He is an unmarried adult male, but is he a bachelor?" Instead, the question is open (nontrivial); so the definition is wrong (Idziak 1979: 19–20).

[15] Atheists could make *negative* moral judgments, like "A isn't good." God's nonexistence would make all negative moral judgments true (see §2.5.1).

regardless of religious beliefs. So believers and atheists seem to mean the same thing by "good." Atheists clearly don't use "good" to mean "desired by God." So, presumably, neither believers nor atheists mean this by "good."

Because of such problems, most DCT thinkers shun the semantic DCT. They see God's will as giving a *criterion* of good but not a *definition* of what "good" means. But will this work?

Suppose that we accept that *a good action is good because God desires it* while claiming that "good" *doesn't mean* "desired by God." We still have to account for the meaning of "good"; what could "good" then mean? Here are three classic views:[16]

1. *Empirical*: "Good" can be defined in descriptive, empirical terms (as perhaps "socially accepted," "what I like," or "what an ideal observer would prescribe"). This makes moral judgments into true-or-false empirical descriptions.
2. *Emotivist*: "Good" expresses feelings: "X is good" means "Hurrah for X!" Moral judgments are exclamations instead of statements that are true or false in a robust sense.
3. *Nonnaturalist*: "Good" can't be defined using descriptive or emotional terms. Moral judgments are objectively true or false; there are independent moral facts that determine the truth or falsity of moral judgments.

None of these fits well with DCT.

The normative DCT holds this:

> A <u>good</u> action is
> <u>good</u> because God desires it.

Can the normative DCT accept the cultural relativist definition of "good" as equivalent to "socially accepted"? Clearly it can't, because then, replacing "good" with its equivalent, the normative DCT would have to mean

> CR: A <u>socially accepted</u> action is
> <u>socially accepted</u> because God desires it.

---

[16] I'm taking "good action" in the sense (whatever that is) that's most common in moral discussions. I take this to be an all-things-considered sense, as contrasted with "good in some respect," "good as a means," or "considered good by a specific group." This is the sense of "good" that I'm seeking to analyze.

But this doesn't make sense. If we try the other empirical definitions of "good" mentioned above, we get further bizarre analyses of what the normative DCT is supposed to mean:

- SB: An action I like is liked by me because God desires it.
- IO: An action that an ideal observer would prescribe would be prescribed by an ideal observer because God desires it.

So these empirical views fit poorly with the normative DCT.

How about emotivism? If we try to replace "good" in the normative DCT with a hurrah exclamation, we get this nonsense:

> EM: An action that is hurrah for this! is hurrah for this! because God desires it.

How about nonnaturalism? Here "good" is indefinable and moral beliefs are made true or false by objective, independent moral facts (and not by God's will). A DCT that held this could regard "*A good action is good because God desires it*" as an objective, irreducible moral truth: it's true, but not because God made it true. However, DCT, which typically dislikes independent moral truths, would likely find this unattractive.

Or we might explain the meaning of "good" by giving a synonym like "commendable" or "desirable." But this is evasive, since it avoids crucial issues about the nature of value. Is "X is commendable" itself a true-or-false empirical description, an expression of feeling, or an irreducible but objective truth claim? Divine-command thinkers need to face these issues.

Normative divine-command thinkers may find that the only meaning analysis of "good" that fits their view is "desired by God." So it's difficult for the normative DCT to avoid the problem-filled semantic DCT. I'll call this the *semantic problem*.

2.6 Knowing God's Will

Suppose God's will determines right and wrong. But then, we have to ask, how can we know God's will? Here are some alternatives. We can know God's will through

1. the Bible
2. the church
3. prayer
4. reason
5. or we cannot know God's will

I'll argue that we need to combine these answers.

(1) *The Bible.* Many people were brought up to believe that the Bible teaches clear answers to all moral issues. But they soon find gray areas where people interpret the Bible differently.

During the Vietnam War, many defended pacifism using the Bible; they believed that it was wrong to kill a human for any reason, even self-defense, and they took "You shall not kill" and "Turn the other cheek" literally. Others, thinking it their duty to fight the "godless Communists," quoted biblical passages urging Israel to conquer its enemies. So should a follower of the Bible be a pacifist or a militarist? We need to understand difficult passages in light of the Bible's general message; but people who try to do this may end up interpreting things differently. So the Bible leaves us with some gray areas. And the Bible doesn't directly address many issues (like atomic weapons).

The Bible testifies that it *isn't* the only way to know right from wrong. First, it speaks of early figures who lived before the Bible was written as knowing about right and wrong. Second, Romans 2:13–15 talks about how nonbelievers can know the moral law (as "written in their hearts").

Which Bible should we follow? Christians, Jews, Muslims, Mormons, and others see different books as revealed. But I'll argue that nearly all religions have the same core ethical message, about loving our neighbor and treating others as we want to be treated. Details vary, but the ethics core is the same.

(2) *The church.* Some see their church as an infallible moral authority; the church teaches an unchanging system of moral truths, and we must accept whatever it says. But history shows that the church can have blind spots (like supporting slavery) and that its teaching has evolved over the years. And so the church for many people is seen, not as the last word on morality, but rather as a wise teacher: we listen and try to learn – but in the end we may disagree on some details.

(3) *Prayer.* Many pray to God for guidance, and then take their feelings as a sign of God's will. While this can lead to virtue if God is seen as loving, there's a danger of confusing our feelings with God's will; religious fanatics may think God wants things that in fact are crazy and hateful. So we need other inputs to help us to form our conscience.

(4) *Reason.* Some follow their moral intuitions, which they see as implanted by God to help us to know his will. Others follow an ideal-observer method, where we try to become as God-like as possible (striving for wisdom and love) and then see what we desire; this gives us an idea of what God would desire. Such approaches can be helpful, especially if we add input from the Bible and the church.

(5) *We cannot know God's will.* Some see God's will as unknowable, since God is mysteriously above our little minds. Romans 11:34 asks, "Who has known the mind of the Lord?" While I see some truth in this, it seems overstated. Surely we know some general things about God's will, even though we can't be sure about all the details.

So how can we know God's will? I suggest that we combine all four sources: the Bible, the church, prayer, and reason.[17] Where the sources speak clearly and in unison, our belief is very solid. So it's clear that God wants us to have concern and love for each other, and to treat others as we want to be treated. It's also clear that God opposes stealing, lying, killing, adultery – and racism (which violates "Love your neighbor"). But there are gray areas, like pacifism. Here we have to follow our prayer and reason as best we can, while we gain insight from the Bible and the church. In these gray areas, we should be less confident of our beliefs and more tolerant of opposing views.

Most religious people, whether or not they accept DCT, want to follow God's will. Most agree that our duty coincides with God's will; but they may disagree on which is the ground of which. Some say that something is our duty because God commands it; others say that God commands something because it's our duty. But both sides can agree that something is our duty if and only if God commands it. Given this, both sides can argue from God's will to duty ("God commands it, so it's our duty") or from duty to God's will ("It's our duty, so God commands it" or "It isn't our duty, so God doesn't command it").

Likewise, some who see God as the ultimate source of morality may also emphasize (as did C. S. Lewis) human reason and conscience as revealing God's will; they may believe that God implanted rules of moral reasoning or even specific moral principles into everyone, including those who never heard of the Bible. And religious people who reject DCT may still look to the Bible for moral insights; they may believe that God has a deeper insight than we do into independent moral truths. So for religious people, their acceptance or rejection of DCT needn't make a big difference in how they come to know right from wrong – or in how they seek to know and follow God's will.

---

[17] *The Spiritual Exercises* of Ignatius of Loyola (1524) gives a multidimensional approach to discerning God's will, and many discussions build on this; Martin (2010) is a good introduction, with further references.

2.7 Further DCT Issues

Now I'll use a question-answer format to explore further issues.

(Q1) What do atheists think of the idea that God is the only possible source of objective moral duties?

A few atheists agree; since they reject God, they then reject objective duties. But most atheists disagree; they contend that atheists can have an adequate morality, and even objective duties, without God. Chapter 7 ("Ethics without God") will discuss atheistic approaches to ethics.

DCT doesn't entail that atheists are evil or can't know right from wrong. DCT could hold, with C. S. Lewis (§2.1), that basic moral norms are built into us and thus known to pretty much everyone, including atheists, who can follow these norms too.

The semantic DCT (§2.5) entails that atheists can't consistently make positive moral judgments; so atheists make such judgments only through conceptual confusion. Some atheists find such DCT forms to be repulsive.

(Q2) Isn't it better to base ethics on something less divisive than religion? Isn't God's will too controversial to lead to a common ethic? (Frankena 1973b)

Some object that, since religions differ much about God's will, DCT leads to a religious moral relativism: *right and wrong are relative to your religion.* So we have Christian ethics, Muslim ethics, Hindu ethics, and so on – each with different values based on a different view of God's will. And subgroups of these, like Baptists and Anglicans, also have different values, as do conservative and liberal Catholics. And DCT leaves out nonbelievers. So DCT divides people.

However, the various faiths share many important norms; the Parliament of the World's Religions in 1993 agreed on the golden rule (GR) and general norms on respecting possessions, speech, life, and family (§5.3). So perhaps we can promote global ethical standards by encouraging each group to understand and live up to its own core values.

(Q3) Doesn't DCT bring narrow-mindedness and bigotry (we favor our group and despise those who are different)? And doesn't it lead people to obey the Bible literally and blindly (authoritarianism), instead of thinking for themselves in a mature way about values (autonomy)?[18]

What DCT leads to depends on God's will. I take God's will to be mostly very general, including norms like GR (to treat *all* others, including those different from us, as we want to be treated) and general norms against stealing, lying, killing, and adultery (which, with GR, are common to the world's religions). Applying these to concrete cases requires intelligence and imagination. And GR doesn't impose a specific rule on us from the outside but rather takes our own rule (e.g., "Don't steal from me!") and pushes us to apply it consistently to how we treat others. So then following God's will leads, not to blind authoritarianism, but to *responsible moral autonomy* – to thinking for ourselves about moral matters in a responsible way.

God can reveal his will about specific matters too. Then, given God's far superior moral wisdom, we should defer to his judgment, *if we can be fairly sure what his will is*. But this problem can arise: we *believe* that God commands A while also *believing* (on seemingly good grounds) that A is wrong. Then we have to decide which of the two beliefs to reject. Are we perhaps mistaken in believing that God commands A? Or are we mistaken in believing that A is wrong (maybe God has reasons that we don't understand)? *We have to make the choice here.*

Beliefs about God's will can be mistaken. Jesus complained that conventional religious rules often twisted God's will, and the same may be true today. Some Christians are judgmental, thinking that this is God's will, even though Jesus forbade this (Matthew 7:1–5). Some Christians hate those who are different, thinking that this is God's will, even though Jesus taught the golden rule and "Love your enemies." Some fundamentalists pick verses of the Bible to take literally but ignore contrary passages and the larger message of God's love. And some take their own opinions about God's will as unquestioned certainties.

Religious moral thinking at its best is *theonomous*: based both on God's will and on a deeper part of our own will that God implanted in us. This is a responsible moral autonomy.[19]

---

[18] Al-Attar (2010), who discusses DCT and its foes in Islam, sees DCT as often being a negative force – but especially when God's will is seen as arbitrary instead of as resting on his wisdom, justice, and love.

[19] For discussions of DCT and moral autonomy, see Adams (1979a, 1979b, 1999: 270–76), Carson (2000: 251), Coulter (1989), Evans (2013: 94–98), Quinn (1978), and

(Q4) Do many DCT views emphasize divine punishments and rewards (including those of the afterlife)?

While these may be more central in the popular understanding, most DCT views don't emphasize rewards and punishments, consider them a high moral motive, or see them as needed for obligations. But a particular DCT view *may* see punishments and rewards as central to morality if it

1. sees moral duties as part of a cosmic legal system and thus as logically requiring an authority who commands and gives penalties for noncompliance; or
2. assumes an egoistic ethics – so our duty is to do what has the best total consequences for us personally; or
3. assumes an egoistic view of human motivation – so our only (or main) motivation is that an action would have the best total consequences for us personally.

William Paley (1743–1805) combined 1 and 3. He saw punishments and rewards as essential for obligations. *Good actions* are ones that promote human happiness; but for such actions to become duties, they must be commanded by God and enforced by afterlife punishments and rewards (which motivate us to act in socially useful ways). Paley defined *virtue* as "doing good to mankind, in obedience to the will of God, and for the sake of everlasting happiness."[20]

(Q5) So some use a nonreligious criterion for distinguishing *good actions*, while basing *duties* on God's will?

Yes. Paley and some other DCT thinkers distinguish "good actions" from "duties." Actions are morally good or bad depending on a non-religious norm (perhaps utilitarian, ideal-observer, or social contract). Morally *good actions* aren't moral *duties* unless we bring in God. Moral *duties* need a *law framework* – a command by God that's backed up by punishments. God is needed to elevate morally *good actions* to the status of moral *duties*; if there were no God, then there'd be morally good actions but no moral duties.[21]

Wainwright (2005: 117–22). Gooch (1983) argues that St. Paul's epistles discuss moral issues in a very nonauthoritarian way.

[20] See Idziak (1979: 214–19). Similar ideas occur in John Gay and, but not as consistently, in John Locke (Idziak 1979: 203–7, 178–88).

[21] Samuel Pufendorf (1632–94) used Hobbesian ideas to pick *moral norms*, as social rules that we'd agree to in the state of nature to help promote the social life that we want for

This modification makes it easier for DCT to deal with some objections (like *Euthyphro*, evil actions, and trivializing God's goodness). But a traditional DCT would complain that it compromises God's sovereignty to have standards of good actions independent of God's will (see §3.3.1).

(Q6) What was Immanuel Kant's view on how divine rewards connect with morality?

Kant (1781: 635–44; 1788: 128–36) argued that practical reason requires belief in freedom, immortality, and God. All are based on the idea that "ought" implies "can" (what we *ought to do* we thereby *can do*). We know that we're free by knowing that we have duties that we violate: we *ought to have acted otherwise*, so we *could have acted otherwise*, and so we're *free*. Further, the *highest good*, which is complete happiness combined with complete good will, *ought to be*, and therefore is possible. But since this highest good isn't possible in the present life, we must assume conditions that make it possible in an afterlife, including the existence of a powerful, moral God who rewards goodness. For Kant, divine reward isn't a proper motive for right action: we're to do the right thing just because it's the right thing. But divine reward is needed if the highest good is to be possible, and morality's coherence requires that the highest good be possible.

We can express Kant's moral argument for God as follows (here "possible" means "factually possible," and "necessary" means "factually necessary"):

People ought to be happy in proportion to their virtue.
What ought to be is possible.
∴ It's possible that people are happy in proportion to their virtue.
Necessarily, if people are happy in proportion to their virtue, then virtuous people will be rewarded either in the present life or in an afterlife.
It isn't possible that virtuous people are rewarded (sufficiently) in the present life.
∴ It's possible that virtuous people are rewarded in an afterlife.
If it's possible that virtuous people are rewarded in an afterlife, then there's a God.
∴ There's a God.

ourselves; but without God's sanctions, moral norms would be useful rules but not laws or duties. Pufendorf insisted that there's no conscience without religion and so the state should punish atheism (which in his time was uncommon). See Gensler and Spurgin (2008: 228–31).

The weakest premise is the second, which applies to ideals that *ought to be*. While many agree that *actions* that we *ought to do* are thus factually possible to do (since we can't have a duty to do the factually impossible), many doubt that the same works for *ideals* that "ought to be." There could be such ideals that can't be actualized. So the argument is questionable.

(Q7) Didn't John Newman also have a moral argument for God's existence?

Yes. Newman (1870: 97–116) saw the clearest sign of God's existence in *conscience* – seen as an emotional reaction to right or wrong, as when we speak of a "guilty conscience." When we do wrong, we experience shame and guilt toward the One to whom we are responsible. Such moral feelings, taken at face value, refer to God as the Supreme Governor and Judge.

Not everyone experiences morality this way; relating moral guilt to God may just come from religious moral training. And this experience, even if universal, could be just a psychological mechanism; it needn't be a reliable sign of a divine lawgiver.

(Q8) Has DCT recently become more popular?

Yes. Among philosophers, DCT has grown in popularity because of increased respect for theism, increased interest in religious issues, and the emergence of modified DCTs.

Robert Adam's (1973) "A modified divine command theory of ethical wrongness" was a breakthrough. While admitting that DCT was widely seen as indefensible, he proposed a modified DCT that he thought *was* defensible. We'll consider such modified DCTs in the next chapter.

Our challenges to DCT involved *Euthyphro*, evil actions, trivializing God's goodness, circularity, atheism, and semantics. Can DCT be modified to overcome such problems? I'll argue that it can. I see two religious views about ethics as defensible: a modified DCT (Chapter 3) and an independent-duties natural law (Chapters 4–6). I'll try to construct the strongest possible view of each type – and then suggest a hybrid view that's even stronger.

3

Modified DCT

This chapter improves divine command theory by adding four words: a good action is good because *a wise and loving* Creator desires it. This modified DCT handles objections better.

Modified DCTs base an action's goodness or rightness on God's will in a qualified way. Recent religious philosophers have developed various modified DCTs.[1] To make the issue more manageable, I'll break the problem of constructing a viable DCT into various subproblems. My goal here is to construct the strongest possible modified DCT.

This chapter rejects *strong moral realism*: it assumes that there are no moral facts about the value of actions (including oughtness, permissibility, and goodness) that hold independently of actual or hypothetical facts about will (desires, commands, approvals, and so on), including divine and human will. Chapters 4–6, about natural law, assume the opposite.

3.1 Qualifications

Suppose there's a personal *Creator* of the world; what qualifications does it need to author the moral order? Consider two cases:

- Creator is *Ares*, like the ancient Greek god of war, but worse. Ares is hateful and loves cruelty. He commands that we hate each other and cause others maximal pain.

---

[1] See my bibliography for Adams, Baggett and Walls, Carson, Evans, J. Hare, Jordan, Quinn, and Wainwright. I'll somewhat follow Carson, who presents the issues very clearly; but I sometimes give his ideas a different twist.

- Creator is *Yahweh*, like the God of Christianity. Yahweh is wise and loving. He commands that we love each other and treat others as we want to be treated.

If the hateful Ares created the world, we'd have no duty to follow his commands; he's unfit to author the moral law. But the wise and loving Yahweh *is* fit to author the moral law.[2] I suggest that Creator, to author the moral law, needs to be like Yahweh: *wise and loving*. So I propose this modified DCT:

> A good action is good because
> a wise and loving Creator desires it.

Love isn't enough, since it could be ignorant. Wisdom isn't enough either, unless it includes love. "Wise and loving" may be enough. Now some atheists may object that our world, with all its suffering, couldn't have come from a wise and loving Creator; we'll deal with this problem in Chapter 8.[3]

3.2 Divine Wisdom

I suggest that the Creator, to author the moral law, has to be *wise* and loving. But what, more precisely, does "wise" here mean? I'll sketch three possible answers.

(1) William Frankena (1973a: 110–14) discusses general moral rationality. He first talks about making evaluative judgments of any sort (including aesthetic, moral, or self-interest ones): we need to be "free, informed, clear-headed, impartial, willing to universalize"[4] – "the question is simply what it is rational to choose" (111). He sometimes says "fully informed" or "informed about all possibly relevant facts" (110, 112). He also includes being able "to realize vividly, in imagination and

---

[2] Bernard Williams (1972) asked which of God's features makes his commands good to follow. Not finding an answer, he concluded that appealing to God adds either *nothing* to morality (if God commands what's already good) or *bad things* (if we obey to avoid punishment). Our modified DCT emphasizes God's supreme *wisdom and love*; these features make his commands good to follow. And §6.5.5 sketches what God adds to morality.

[3] I use "Creator" in much of this chapter, instead of "God," to avoid verbal issues that come from different understandings of the term "God" (e.g., as entailing or not entailing being supremely wise and loving).

[4] By "willing to universalize" Frankena (1973a: 25) means *willing to make the same evaluative judgment about the same kind of case*. I take *impartial* (which he doesn't further explain) to be the same thing.

feeling, the 'inner lives' of others" (79). Following this, a "wise" Creator is one who is *free, fully and vividly informed about all possibly relevant facts, clear-headed, impartial, and willing to universalize.*[5]

(2) Thomas Carson (2000: 250; 2012: 458–59) begins the summary of his modified DCT as follows:

> If there is an omniscient God who designed and created the universe and human beings for certain purposes/reasons, who cares deeply about human beings, and is kind, sympathetic, and unselfish..., then God's preferences are the ultimate standard for the correctness/rationality of human preferences and for the goodness or badness of things.

If we split this, we can put "omniscient, sympathetic, and unselfish" (and maybe more) under "wise," and the rest under "loving" (in the next section). Carson (2000: 224, 242) takes *omniscience* to include an ideal vividness of knowledge and thus a vivid understanding of the feelings of others. So then a "wise" Creator is perhaps one who *knows every truth vividly, accepts no falsehoods, and is sympathetic and unselfish.*

(3) My ethics textbook (Gensler 2011a: 97–99) suggests that we're rational in our moral thinking to the extent that we're consistent, informed, imaginative, and a few more things. My "informed and imaginative" is like Frankena's "fully and vividly informed" and Carson's "vivid understanding." My "a few more things" has items less relevant here, like "Feel free to think for yourself (and not just conform)."

My consistency condition prescribes (§§4.3–4.4) the following:

- *Consistency in beliefs*: Don't accept logically incompatible beliefs, and don't accept a belief without also accepting its logical consequences.
- *Consistency of will*: Don't have incompatible all-things-considered desires; don't have resolutions that conflict with actions; and don't combine having an end, believing that achieving this end requires carrying out certain means, and not carrying out the means.
- *Conscientiousness*: Keep your actions, resolutions, and desires in harmony with your moral beliefs.
- *Impartiality*: Make similar evaluations about similar actions, regardless of the individuals involved.[6]

---

[5] Frankena (1973a: 113) adds that for *moral* judgments we also need to take into account the good or evil done to other sentient beings. Perhaps a "loving" Creator must care about the good or evil done to any sentient creature.

[6] Impartiality here is judging consistently about similar cases. I can judge that *I ought to show greater concern for my children* so long as I judge that in similar cases *others ought to show greater concern for their children.*

- *Golden rule*: Treat others only as you consent to being treated in the same situation.

How would these apply to the Creator?

- *Consistency in beliefs*: An *omniscient* Creator would automatically avoid inconsistency in beliefs.
- *Consistency of will*: A Creator needs to avoid contradictory commands (which give a poor basis for duties) and having an end but not carrying out the necessary means.
- *Conscientiousness*: An omniscient Creator whose will creates the moral order will automatically have his will be in harmony with his moral beliefs.
- *Impartiality*: A Creator needs to create moral standards that generate similar evaluations about similar actions, regardless of the individuals involved.
- *Golden rule*: A Creator needs to treat creatures only as he consents to being treated in the same situation (in which he imagines himself being such a creature).

This view suggests that a "wise" Creator is one who is *maximally consistent, informed, and imaginative*.

So how do we explain "wise" in our modified DCT? I've sketched three possible analyses (based on Frankena, Carson, and Gensler). A *wise* Creator is one who

- is free, fully and vividly informed about all possibly relevant facts, clear-headed, impartial, and willing to universalize
- knows every truth vividly, accepts no falsehoods, and is sympathetic and unselfish
- is maximally consistent, informed, and imaginative

These could be combined or tweaked further. I'm less concerned with details than with the general idea.

3.3 Divine Love

I suggest that the Creator, to author the moral law, has to be wise and *loving*. But what, more precisely, does "loving" here mean? I'll again sketch three possible answers.

"Loving another" here means "desiring and seeking the other's good."[7] So perhaps a *loving* Creator inherently desires the good of every sentient being, doesn't inherently desire harm to any such being, and tolerates harm to such beings only for the sake of their greater good. Here I take "desire" to include *seeking after*. Creator must desire *everyone's* good; desiring the good of only some can lead to acting wrongly toward others.

But this leads to circularity: we explain "good" using "wise and loving," and then explain "loving" using "good." I'll sketch three ways to handle this circularity problem.

(1) A *mixed approach* avoids circularity by having one type of good depend on another type. The *intrinsic-values type of good*, which the notion of a "loving Creator" presupposes, is objective and independent of the Creator's will. But the *action type of good* depends on the will of a wise and loving Creator, and thus indirectly on the intrinsic-values type of good.[8]

Philosophical questions about "the good" are about *the goodness of a life*. What in life is valuable, or worth being sought? What constitutes our well-being? *Hedonism* says pleasure is the good; but *pluralism* says there are several ultimate goods, like virtue, knowledge, pleasure, life, and freedom. How do we know the good? Some appeal to moral intuitions, while others appeal to what we'd desire for ourselves if we were wise or rational (informed, consistent, imaginative, and so on).[9]

Suppose that we have a view of intrinsic value and the good life. Various views about good or obligatory *actions* are compatible with this, for example,

- *Egoism*: We ought to maximize the balance of good over harm for ourselves, regardless of how this affects others.
- *Act utilitarianism*: We ought to do whatever act maximizes the total balance of good over harm for everyone.

---

[7] See Carson (2000: 246–48; 2012: 466). The love-your-neighbor kind of "love" is also called *agape* (ἀγάπη in Greek), as opposed to *eros* (ἔρως, erotic love) and *filia* (φιλία, friendship).

[8] Adams (1973, 1979a, 1999), Alston (2002), Evans (2013), Kaye (2003), and Wainright (2005) want duty to depend on God's will but goodness to be either independent of God or else depend on imitating God's nature. On this view, God commands A *because* A is good, and the command raises A to a duty.

[9] For more on intrinsic value and the good life, see Carson (2000) Frankena (1973a: 79–94), and Gensler 2011a: (116–20).

- *Rule utilitarianism*: We ought to follow whatever social rules would, if people tried to follow them, maximize the total balance of good over harm for everyone.
- *Nonconsequentialism*: Other things equal, we ought to avoid harming others (a very stringent duty), bring good to others, return good to those who have brought us good, make up for harm we've brought to others, and so on.

So an intrinsic-values view doesn't itself determine which actions are right or wrong or how we ought to live.

On this mixed DCT, there are objective truths about intrinsic good and bad that aren't based on God's will. But Creator, given that he's loving (= *cares about the good or bad done to all sentient beings*), decides through his will which *actions* will be good or bad and how we ought to live. So we avoid circularity by having one type of good depend on another; the goodness of actions depends, through the will of a wise and loving creator, on independent truths about intrinsic values.

The main problem with this mixed DCT is the tension between its parts (Kaye 2003). If *objective moral laws* require a source, then why don't *objective intrinsic values* require a source? If *duties* independent of God's will violate his sovereignty, then why don't *intrinsic values* independent of his will do this too? Reasons to prefer a religious basis for *duty* are also reasons to prefer a religious basis for *intrinsic value*. So this mixed approach has problems.

(2) We might avoid circularity by explaining "loving" without appealing to antecedent intrinsic values. Instead of saying that Creator is "loving," Carson (2000: 248–50; 2012: 458–59) says that he "cares deeply about human beings, and is kind, sympathetic, and unselfish." He tries to explain these notions without assuming value notions.[10]

Carson proposes that the Creator must, to be the ultimate standard for goodness and badness, care very deeply about human beings, and this for our own sake; he isn't coldhearted and indifferent to us. He's kind and sympathetic, being pleased by our joy and distressed by our suffering; he doesn't take cruel delight in our suffering – but he may permit suffering for higher goals and for our sake. While I'm not sure that all these terms

---

[10] Carson sees this longer phrase as replacing rather than explaining the "loving" clause. He also discusses exemplarist approaches of Adams and Zagzebski that try to deal with the circularity problem.

are value neutral (especially "care about" and "kind"), it does seem to me that this approach can work.[11]

(3) We might avoid circularity by explaining "loving" as *following the golden rule* (GR).[12] This has the Creator treating creatures only as he consents to being treated in the same situation (in which he imagines himself being such a creature). This explanation doesn't use evaluative terms and so doesn't bring circularity. Wisdom, if taken to include the consistency sketched in §3.2, requires following GR; so then this GR condition wouldn't have to be added to wisdom, but only seen as a consequence of wisdom.

Some may see this idea – of Creator following GR toward us – as unfamiliar and bizarre. But that's not an argument. In fact, it's difficult to come up with a solid objection to the idea. The idea makes sense to me.

So how do we explain "loving" in our modified DCT? I've sketched three possible analyses. A *loving* Creator is one who

- cares about the good or bad done to any sentient being (where "good and bad" are intrinsic values independent of the Creator's will)
- cares deeply about human beings and is kind, sympathetic, and unselfish (where these terms are taken to not assume value notions)
- follows the GR toward his creatures

These could be combined or tweaked further. I conclude that our modified DCT ("A good action is good because a wise and loving Creator desires it") is workable, even though thinkers may explain "wise" and "loving" differently.[13]

3.4 Atheists

Our modified DCT bases the good/bad action distinction on a *wise and loving Creator*. But what about atheists? Should those who reject a

---

[11] Carson's approach uses a thin theory of the good – whereby we speak of joy and suffering instead of good and bad. While a theist will likely reject hedonism (§§8.1–8.3), here it may suffice to just mention joy and suffering.

[12] St. Thomas Aquinas (1274, I–II, q. 99, a. 1) and others explain neighborly love as treating our neighbor as we want to be treated (Gensler 2013: 39). But I've never heard of anyone explaining God's love for us as treating us only as he's willing to be treated in the same situation. I don't see this as the whole analysis of what it means to say that God loves us; but it may capture enough of the "loving" idea to provide a suitable substitute in this context.

[13] God's wisdom and love likely go far beyond what we can conceive. Our explanations give only minimal requirements for authoring the moral law.

Creator also reject the good/bad action distinction and so reject morality? Or is morality about which actions flow from *wisdom and love*, which atheists can accept too, with a *Creator* being irrelevant? How can modified DCT let atheists into the moral door without making God irrelevant to morality?

Atheists can be good and moral people; this is a clear fact of our experience. This presents problems for traditional (§2.7.1) and modified DCTs. When combined with an atheistic premise that denies the existence of a God or Creator, both DCTs, depending on their wording, may logically entail conclusions like "All actions are permissible – there are no duties" or "No actions are objectively good or bad." These conclusions clash with the moral beliefs and practice of most atheists.

DCT can respond in either of two ways. First, it might say that atheists can be good and moral, but only if they don't clearly understand what morality is about. If atheists understood things better, they'd realize that atheism is incompatible with morality; so they'd need to choose to keep atheism (and reject morality) or keep morality (and reject atheism).

Or DCT could add an escape clause (here italicized):

> *If there's a God, then* a good action is good because
> God desires it; *if there's no God, then the goodness*
> *of actions is determined in some other way.*

This escape clause lets atheists have a genuine morality.[14] It also suggests that the two groups may live in very different moral universes and may have little common ground for discussing moral issues or cooperating on moral projects (like peace and justice). This is an unhappy result.

Our modified DCT, however, can bring common ground. Theists and atheists can agree: "Morality needs to be based on wisdom and love." But whose wisdom and love? Who decides right and wrong? Clearly the highest available wisdom and love should decide this. If there exists an infinite wisdom and love (God), then he should decide right and wrong. But if the highest available wisdom and love is that of humans, then human wisdom and love should decide right and wrong.

And so my further modified DCT asserts,

Right and wrong should be decided by the highest available wisdom and love. This is either God (if he exists and is wise and loving) or human wisdom and love (otherwise).

---

[14] Carson (2012: 459; 2000: 250) uses an escape clause. Adams (1973), Zagzebski (2004), and others use other devices to let atheists make moral judgments.

Theists and atheists could agree on these ideas and thus inhabit adjacent parts of a wisdom-and-love moral universe; instead of two radically different schemes, we'd have infinite and finite variations on the same theme. Believers base right/wrong on the will of a wise and loving God; atheists can concede that this *would* be a suitable basis for morality *if* there were such a God. Atheists base right/wrong on human wisdom and love; believers can concede that this *would* be a suitable basis for morality *if* there were no wise and loving God. The overlap in ideas helps both sides to discuss moral issues and cooperate on moral projects. So this modified DCT could appeal to both groups.

Divine-command thinkers may object that this scheme puts divine and human wisdom on an equal footing. But the two are decidedly unequal: even at its best, human wisdom is only a dim reflection of divine wisdom. Defining right/wrong by divine wisdom is straightforward; but defining it by human wisdom, while possible, is a can of worms.

Frankena (§3.2) and others require that, in making evaluative judgments, *we be fully and vividly informed about all possibly relevant facts*. This would be physically impossible for small-brained creatures like ourselves, even if we did nothing else but think about ethical issues. Carson (2012: 468) writes,

Being fully informed, or even possessing all relevant information, greatly exceeds human capacities. It is impossible for any human being to possess all the information relevant to . . . my choice of careers (having all information relevant to those questions would require having a vivid knowledge of what my life and life history would have been like if I had pursued any one of the thousands of different careers I might have chosen). Because of this, counterfactual statements of the sort upon which such theories of rationality depend, e.g. "if I were fully informed, vividly aware of all relevant information, then I would (would not) prefer career X to career Y," have no determinate truth value, indeed the antecedents of such statements are arguably incoherent. . . .

My divine preference theory of rationality avoids all of these problems. Being fully informed does not exceed God's capacities. . . . [These problems] point us strongly in the direction of the divine will theory of rationality. The notion of an ideally rational human being is deeply problematic, but if there exists a God of the sort described by my theory, then God *is* the ideal observer.

Following what we humans would desire if we were "*fully and vividly informed about all possibly relevant facts*" faces further problems (see Carson 2000: 222–39):

- Issues may involve an almost endless sequence of pros and cons, and our preferences about what to do may keep switching back and forth as we gain more and more facts.
- The order in which we vividly reflect on the facts may influence which alternative we finally prefer.
- As we gain more and more facts, and vividly reflect on these, we may suffer *cognitive overload*, becoming depressed, bitter, confused, or unable to think.
- Creatures with brains big enough to avoid such problems would differ much from us in biology and desires. And such brains might not be biologically possible.
- Even humans with ideal information and rationality may disagree, since they may weigh factors differently, like well-being versus freedom. So human rationality may lead to much relativism about right and wrong.
- There are conflicting views about what the idealized conditions for rational choice are; which should we follow?

To deal with such problems, Carson (2000: 232) considers a nonreligious understanding of *rational human preference*; it defines "It's correct for S to prefer X to not-X" this way:

There is at least one empirically possible cognitive/informational perspective (P1) from which S would prefer X to not-X and there is no other empirically possible perspective (P2) which is as good or better than P1 (for deciding between X and not-X) such that S would not prefer X to not-X from P2.

Carson sees this as unclear and messy (2000: 232–34), and he prefers the divine-preference account.

Using divine preferences avoids these problems. God can vividly know all facts without cognitive overload and can satisfy any plausible rationality conditions. God's preferences would give an objective, nonrelativistic, single answer about moral issues, instead of the conflicting answers that idealized human rationality may lead to. So morality on the divine-rationality view is *well defined* (in that controversial moral questions can have a right answer) and thus more *objective*.

3.5 Command or Desire

So far, we've been sloppy about evaluative terms (like "good," "right," and "ought") and matching volitional terms (like "command," "desire," and "prefer"). Now we'll get clearer.

We characterize actions morally using different kinds of moral terms. First are *deontic terms*, such as these three:

- "Ought" ("morally required," "obligatory")
- "wrong"
- "right" ("morally permissible," "all right")

These are interdefinable (here A stands for an action, like *your reading this book*):

- A is obligatory = not-A is wrong = not-A isn't permissible
- A is wrong = A isn't permissible = not-A is obligatory
- A is permissible = A isn't wrong = not-A isn't obligatory

DCT would give these equivalents (assume that God exists as the wise and loving Creator):

- A is obligatory = God commands A[15]
- A is wrong = God forbids A = God commands not-A
- A is permissible = God doesn't forbid A
- A is neither obligatory nor wrong = God neither commands A nor forbids A

The next two sections will consider how to interpret " =."

The main *axiological terms* are "good" and "bad"; these can be strengthened, weakened, and compared, as in "very good," "slightly bad," and "better than." Here are DCT equivalents:

- A is good = God desires (endorses, approves, favors) A
- A is bad = God opposes (is against) A
- A is very good = God greatly desires A
- A is slightly bad = God slightly opposes A
- A is better than B = God prefers A to B
- A is neither good nor bad = God neither desires nor opposes A = God is neutral about A

A good act needn't be obligatory (since God might desire it but not command it); and a bad act needn't be wrong (God might oppose but not forbid it).

"Praiseworthy" and "blameworthy" evaluate *why* the act is done, while "good" and "bad" often evaluate just *what* is done. We might say, "He freed his slaves, not because he cared for them, but because he

---

[15] Perhaps "commands" sounds dictatorial and "God calls upon us to do A" may be better. But here I'll keep to the traditional wording.

feared a violent uprising; his freeing of them was *a good action but not praiseworthy – what* he did was good but not *why* he did it." Here are DCT equivalents:

- Your act A is praiseworthy = Your motives for doing A accord with God's desires about your motives
- Your act A is blameworthy = Your motives for doing A clash with God's desires about your motives

A *supererogatory action* is one that's very good and praiseworthy but not obligatory. In Matthew 19:21, Jesus tells the rich young man, "If you want to be perfect, sell all your possessions, give the money to the poor, and follow me as a disciple." I conjecture that this proposed action is permissible but not obligatory, and that it's very good (and very praiseworthy). In DCT language: God neither commands nor forbids it, but he much desires it (and the motives that you'd have for doing it).

The main controversy is whether to define deontic notions (like "ought," "right," and "wrong") using *commands*, as earlier, or using *desires or preferences*. Adams (1999: 258–70) defends *commands*, since this lets God desire some actions without making them obligatory; explaining "A is obligatory" as "God desires A" makes this (and supererogatory actions) impossible. Adams sees a divine command as a speech act that communicates the divine will to creatures. A legislator's will imposes no obligations unless it's communicated; and so it's God's command, not his desire, that imposes obligations. God communicates commands through conscience (intuitive principles or moral reasoning), social norms (religious or secular), prayer, biblical injunctions, and direct revelation.

Carson (2012: 466–67) doubts that divine commands have been effectively communicated, as is needed to impose duties.[16] He suggests a complex analysis of duties. To make A obligatory, God must prefer A *and either* feel angry about omitting A *or* prefer that omitting A bring guilt-and-remorse to the agent and resentment-and-disapproval from others. This allows for supererogatory actions and good actions that aren't duties.

A third alternative is to define deontic terms by talking about what God requires, permits, approves, or disapproves:

- A is obligatory = God inwardly requires A (God inwardly disapproves of not-A)

---

[16] See also Evans (2013: 37–45) and Jordan (2012, 2013b).

- A is wrong = God inwardly requires not-A (God inwardly disapproves of A)
- A is permissible = God inwardly permits A (God inwardly approves of A)

"Inwardly" expresses that God needn't communicate his will to creatures. Since God may desire actions that he doesn't require, this view allows for good actions that aren't obligations.

I won't take a stand on which option is best. I'll speak vaguely of "God's will" and let people interpret this as they like.

3.6 Definitions

Suppose we accept a *modified normative DCT*, as sketched so far in this chapter:

> If there's a wise and loving Creator, then a good action
> is good because this Creator desires it.

I'll argue for basing this on a definition of "good action."

A *definition* is a rule of paraphrase intended to explain meaning (Gensler 2010: 36–43). More fully, a *definition* of a word or phrase is a rule saying how to eliminate this word or phrase in any sentence and produce a second sentence that means the same thing, the purpose of this being to explain or clarify the meaning of the term. Definitions should avoid circularity, use clear language, and let us paraphrase out the defined term. Definitions can be *analyzing* (explain current usage), *stipulative* (specify how you're going to use a term), or *clarifying* (specify a clearer meaning for a vague term).

(1) An *analyzing definition* is a rule of paraphrase intended to explain current usage. Consider these analyzing definitions of "bachelor" (meant to explain the marital-status sense and not the sense used in "bachelor of arts"):

A. "Bachelor" means "happy man."
B. "Bachelor" means "unmarried man."
C. "Bachelor" means "unmarried male who is at least eighteen."

We can test a definition by switching the terms in a variety of contexts to see if the resulting pair of sentences mean the same thing. Definition A is flawed, since we can consistently claim that John is a <u>bachelor</u> but isn't a happy man, or that John is a happy man but isn't a bachelor; so "John is a bachelor" and "John is a happy man" don't mean the same thing.

Definition B survives the test. Using it on "John is a bachelor," we get "John is an unmarried man" as equivalent; the two seem to have the same meaning and be true in the same cases.

Definition C is flawed because "at least eighteen" is overly precise. A good analyzing definition matches in vagueness the term defined. The ordinary sense of "bachelor" is vague, since the age where it first applies is unclear on semantic grounds. So "over eighteen" is too precise to define the ordinary sense of "bachelor." "Man" or "adult" are better choices, since these match "bachelor" fairly well in vagueness.

Definition C, however, might be a good *clarifying definition* for certain purposes. If we do an empirical study comparing the income of bachelors and nonbachelors, we'd need to stipulate some age (perhaps eighteen or twenty-one) at which we'd consider bachelorhood to begin. We'd pick the age on practical grounds, to enhance the value of the study.

Consider these two analyzing definitions of "good action" (meant to explain the moral sense of *good action*):

A.   "Good action" means "action approved by our society."
B.   "Good action" means "action that would be endorsed by the highest intelligence and concern for everyone."

Definition A is flawed, since we can consistently claim that a racist action approved by our society isn't a good action. So "action approved by our society" and "good action" don't mean the same thing.

Definition B better captures the ordinary meaning of "good action." Paraphrasing "Racist actions aren't good" as "Racist actions wouldn't be endorsed by the highest intelligence and concern for others" is plausible and more informative than replacing "good" with "commendable" or "virtuous."

One might object that definition B carries no inherent motivation, since one might not care about what would be endorsed by the highest intelligence and concern. But almost everyone has *some* motivation to follow this; society teaches us to think before we act and to have concern for others, and evolution may have built this into us too (Gensler 2013: 66).

One might object that definition B is vague and lacks philosophical precision. But this vagueness is a virtue, since the ordinary-language sense of "good action" would be unlikely to have high philosophical precision.

(2) A *stipulative definition* specifies how you're going to use a term. Since your usage may be a new one, it's unfair to criticize a stipulative definition for clashing with current usage. Stipulative definitions should be judged, not as correct or incorrect, but rather as useful or useless. My logic textbook (Gensler 2010) has stipulative definitions for terms like "argument," "valid," and "wff"; these create a technical vocabulary.

Consider these stipulative definitions of "rational action":

A. "Rational$_1$ action" means "emotionless action."
B. "Rational$_2$ action" means "action that effectively promotes your desires."
C. "Rational$_3$ action" means "action that's informed and satisfies golden-rule consistency (you're willing that you'd be treated the same way in the same circumstances)."

A philosophy paper might distinguish such senses to contrast different types of rationality.

Suppose we think the ordinary usage of "good action" is hopelessly confused. Then we might *stipulate* our own sense of "good action," which we claim to be clearer and to satisfy the purposes for which people use moral language; we might try to get people to use "good action" in our proposed sense.[17] A less cynical approach would see the ordinary use of "good action" as genuine but vague; philosophy could then propose a *clarifying definition* of "good action" that builds on ordinary language but is clearer and better satisfies the purposes for which people use moral language. This is the approach that I'll take here.

(3) A *clarifying definition* is one that stipulates an improved and clearer meaning for a vague term. Consider these clarifying definitions of "pure water":

A. "Pure water" means "water you can safely drink."
B. "Pure water" means "water with a 99.9 percent removal or inactivation of giardia, a 99.99 percent removal or inactivation of viruses, and so on." (The EPA standard starts this way.)
C. "Pure water" means "distilled water."

---

[17] Richard Brandt, a teacher of mine at Michigan, sometimes spoke this way: ethical theory should propose a *replacement* for the usual moral terms. But he sometimes spoke more along the lines of clarifying definitions: ethical theory should propose *clearer versions* of the usual moral terms.

Definition B, which gives testable characteristics to minimize health haz-
ards, is more scientifically precise than definition A. Definition C gives a
still higher standard. Other definitions of "pure water" can be developed
for other purposes (like humidifiers). So a *clarifying definition* gives a
more precise analogue, for human purposes, of a vague term like "pure
water."

I suggested that the ordinary meaning of "(morally) good action" is
something like "action that would be endorsed by the highest intelligence
and concern for everyone." Philosophical reflection can lead us to sharpen
this definition; so we might add "vivid awareness" and "consistency" to
the "highest intelligence" part, and we might add GR consistency (that we
act only as we're willing that we'd be treated in the same circumstances)
to the "concern for everyone" part. Earlier (§§3.2–3.3), we specified
enhanced senses of "wisdom" and "love" that include such refinements.
Building on these, I propose this *clarifying definition* of "(morally) good
action":

> "Good action" means "action desired by
> the highest available wisdom and love."

This builds on the ordinary-language meaning of "good action" but clarifies this meaning to better fulfill its built-in goals (to use intelligence to
promote concern for all).

As before (§3.4), this definition can be applied in two ways. Believers
can argue this way:

> Good action = action desired by the highest available wisdom and
> love. (true by definition)
> The highest available wisdom and love = the wise and loving Creator.
> (factual premise accepted by believers)
> ∴ Good action = action desired by the wise and loving Creator.

The DCT conclusion follows by substituting identicals. This conclusion
isn't true by definition; instead, it's true because of a definition plus a
factual premise.

Atheists can argue this way:

> Good action = action desired by the highest available wisdom and
> love. (true by definition)
> The highest available wisdom and love = human wisdom and love.
> (factual premise accepted by atheists)
> ∴ Good action = action desired by human wisdom and love.

The humanistic conclusion follows by substituting identicals.

This approach gives a strong defense of DCT for believers while also allowing atheists to have a humanistic ethics.

3.7 Property Identity

The DCT camp has shifted from meaning ("'Good' means...") to properties ("The property of goodness is identical to..."). Again, Robert Adams (1979a: 66, 76) led the change:

> My [earlier] modified divine command theory was proposed as a partial analysis of the meaning of "(ethically) wrong."... My new divine command theory... is that ethical wrongness *is* (i.e. is identical with) the property of being contrary to the commands of a loving God. I regard this as a metaphysically necessary, but not an analytic or *a priori* truth. Because it is not a conceptual analysis, this claim is not relative to a religious sub-community of the larger linguistic community. It purports to be the correct theory of the nature of the ethical wrongness that *everybody* (or almost everybody) is talking about.

Metaphysical property analysis soon became the new DCT orthodoxy.[18] To explain it, advocates use a "water = H_2O" example from Hilary Putnam (1973) and Saul Kripke (1972).

Water, the common liquid that fills lakes and streams, is a "natural kind": a kind of thing we *discover* in nature as existing independently of us – as opposed to beer or buildings or political boundaries, which we *impose* on nature. We discovered the *nature* of water, that water is H_2O. This discovery is factual, not semantic. "Water" (a colorless, tasteless, good-to-drink liquid plentiful on our planet) and "H_2O" (a molecule composed of two hydrogen atoms and one oxygen atom) have different meanings; but the property of being water = the property of being H_2O. The "water = H_2O" identity, while not analytic (true by definition), is metaphysically necessary (holds in every possible world). If we went to another planet, like Twin Earth, and found a liquid that looked, tasted, and was used like water but had a different chemical constitution, then this liquid definitely *wouldn't* be water, because it has a different nature.

Likewise, moral philosophy needs to study not *the meaning of "good"* but *the nature of goodness*. It needs to complete the sentence "The property of goodness is identical to..." The new DCT proposes that *the property of goodness* is identical to *the property of being desired by God*.

---

[18] See Adams (1979a, 1999), Alston (2002), J. Hare (2001, 2006), Jordan (2012, 2013b), Wainwright (2005), and Zagzebski (2004). Boyd (1988) and many others identify moral properties with empirical properties (§7.2).

This DCT is about metaphysical identity, not meaning identity. Atheists who attribute goodness to actions don't *mean* "good" in the sense of "desired by God"; but, unknown to them, the property of goodness is identical to the property of being desired by God.

I'll argue that this is based on confusion. I'll give four problems:

(1) I reflected on this "water = H_2O" identity while backpacking in the Grand Canyon. At my campsite, I filled my water bottle from Hance Creek, straining out tadpoles with my bandana, and I started to purify the water. But if water = H_2O, then purifying the water would be a waste of time:

> Water = H_2O.
> All H_2O is colorless, tasteless, and good to drink.
> ∴ All water is colorless, tasteless, and good to drink.

Premise 1 is the *water = H_2O* idea. Premise 2 is a truth about H_2O; if you take just H_2O and put it in a clean empty bottle, the contents will be colorless, tasteless, and good to drink. The conclusion follows using a recognized principle of identity logic (Gensler 2010: 205–12) that equals may substitute for equals.[19] Since I had doubts about the argument, I purified the water and so protected myself from maybe getting sick through giardia.

Later I rejected premise 1 (*water = H_2O*) on the basis that H_2O and water often have different properties. H_2O is always colorless, tasteless, and good to drink. But water, as found in nature, isn't always colorless, tasteless, and good to drink. In the Grand Canyon, the Havasu River is deep blue, the Little Colorado River is milky blue, and the Colorado River is green or brown, depending on flooding of side canyons. Variable too is taste (Little Colorado River water is disgusting and ocean water is salty) and suitability for drinking (Horn Creek is radioactive and ocean water is too salty to drink). So we can argue

> All H_2O is colorless, tasteless, and good to drink.
> Not all water is colorless, tasteless, and good to drink.
> ∴ Water ≠ H_2O.

If we assume the falsity of the conclusion, we can get a contradiction by exchanging "water" and "H_2O" in either premise.

---

[19] *Interchangeability of identicals* is the clearest point about identity (although it needs to be qualified in belief and other intensional contexts). Rejecting this would leave identity without any clear meaning.

Water, as a natural-kind liquid, is always a *mixture* of various things, with H_2O being the major part; it's never just *identical* to H_2O. Water, as found in nature, contains hundreds of ingredients and is varied in composition and properties. H_2O isn't so varied. Even *pure water* (§3.6.3) is a mixture, and not just identical to H_2O; even the purest multiply distilled water that we can produce is a mixture, containing much HO and H_3O.

The only way to make "water = H_2O" true is to use "water" in an artificially simplified way that likely refers to no existing liquid – as meaning "a liquid containing only H_2O." This makes "water = H_2O" true by definition, which defeats the example's purpose: to find a natural kind with an identity that's metaphysically necessary but *not* true by definition.

I don't object to young children learning the oversimplified idea that water is H_2O. But later they should learn that the common liquid we call "water" is a *mixture*, with H_2O the major ingredient but with further ingredients that determine whether the water is salt or fresh, good to drink or not, clear or murky, alkaline or acidic, and so on.

(2) How do problems with the "water = H_2O" example affect DCT? Well, property identity is traditionally determined by semantics: property F is identical to property G, if and only if the term expressing property F has the same meaning as the term expressing G. The "water = H_2O" example gives a major objection to this semantic view of property identity.

This traditional view contrasts *sets* with *properties*. A *set*, roughly, is a collection of things; two sets with the same members are considered to be identical. Suppose that all and only beings with hearts also have kidneys. Then the set of beings with hearts = the set of beings with kidneys. In general, set a = set b if and only if set a and set b have the same members.

A *property*, roughly, is a characteristic distinguishing one kind of thing from another. *How* a property picks things out (and not just the set of things it picks out) is essential. So identity of properties requires sameness of meaning. The property of having a heart ≠ the property of having a kidney, since "X has a heart" isn't synonymous with "X has a kidney"; we can consistently, in terms of logic and semantics, imagine one true but not the other. In general, property F = property G, if and only if "X is F" is synonymous with "X is G."[20]

---

[20] Quine (1986: 67, 8–10) uses this heart/kidney example to contrast identity conditions for sets and properties. Quine abhors properties and synonymy; but he well explains the traditional semantic approach to property identity.

Consider these three pairs of statements, divided into semantic and property versions:

1s. "Good action" means "action approved by our society."
1p. The property of being a good action = the property of being approved by our society.
2s. "Good action" means "action desired by God."
2p. The property of being a good action = the property of being desired by God.
3s. "Water" means "H_2O."
3p. The property of being water = the property of being H_2O.

On the traditional semantic approach to property identity, the consistency of "Racist actions approved by our society aren't necessarily good" refutes 1s and 1p (cultural relativism), the consistency of "There may exist good actions but no God" refutes 2s and 2p (DCT), and the consistency of "There could be water with a different chemical analysis than H_2O" refutes 3s and 3p.

The "water = H_2O" example attacks this traditional semantic approach to property identity. It argues that "water" and "H_2O" differ in meaning (making 3s false), but yet the property of being water = the property of being H_2O (making 3p true). So property identity doesn't depend on meaning identity. Thus we *can't* refute claims about property identity by pointing out that certain claims are (semantically) consistent.

Many DCT defenders like this result, since then a standard argument against DCT (as 2p) fails. But then, alas, a great argument against cultural relativism (as 1p) also fails. More generally, we can, without fear of being refuted, say almost anything we want about what the property of goodness is identical to; there's no strong way to argue about property identity. Some DCT defenders like this, perhaps because they don't want to *argue* for their view against opposing views.

The water example tries to refute the semantic approach to property identity. It argues that water = H_2O while yet "water" and "H_2O" differ in meaning. But does this example take "water" in the ordinary sense (as a natural-kind liquid found in nature)? Then water isn't identical to H_2O but rather is a *mixture* containing H_2O and other things. Or does it take "water" in an artificially simplified sense (as "a liquid containing only H_2O")? Taking "water" in this sense, "water = H_2O" is *true by definition*. Thus the water objection to the semantic approach to property identity fails.

(3) The "water = H_2O" identity is an empirical claim about chemical composition; but DCT isn't anything like this. So the analogy is strained and does little to help us understand DCT.

(4) A DCT that expresses itself in terms of property identity still needs to talk about the *meaning* of "good." (Analogously, if we hold that water = H_2O, we still need to talk about the *meaning* of "water.") Section 2.5 showed that this is difficult to do in a way that's congenial to DCT. But our previous section points to a very workable way to build DCT on an understanding of what "good" means.

Here's a better way to argue for a property DCT. Assume our clarifying definition: "good action" means "action desired by the highest available wisdom and love." Using the semantic property-identity view, derive this: "The property of being a good action = the property of being an action desired by the highest available wisdom and love." Substitute identicals in a logical truth ("An action has the property of being a good action, if and only if it has the property of being a good action") to get this: "An action has the property of being a good action, if and only if it has the property of being an action desired by the highest available wisdom and love." Using "God = the highest available wisdom and love," substitute identicals again to get this: "An action has the property of being a good action, if and only if it has the property of being an action desired by God."

3.8 Answering Objections

I'll now try to show that our modified DCT can deal well with the objections to the traditional DCT, as raised in Chapter 2.

(*Euthyphro* question, §2.3) Is a good action good because God desires it? Or does God desire it because it's good?

The first option is the right one, *given the assumption that God is the highest available wisdom and love*. Then, from "Kindness is desired by God," we can derive "Kindness is good":

> Kindness is desired by God.
> God is the highest available wisdom and love.
> ∴ Kindness is desired by the highest available wisdom and love.
> ∴ Kindness is good. (by our definition of "good action")

If premise 2 is false, and so something other than God is the highest available wisdom and love, then actions are good because this something else desires them.

(Evil-actions objection, §2.3) If actions are good just because God desires them, then continually hating others would be good if God desired it. But clearly such hatred wouldn't be good even if God desired it. So actions aren't good just because God desires them.

God's will wouldn't decide what is good if God were unloving – desiring continual hatred, for example. God needs to be *wise and loving* for his will to make actions good or bad.

The desires of a wise and loving God could be arbitrary to some extent – not to the extent of desiring continual hatred but to the extent of desiring that we worship him in a special way on a certain arbitrarily selected day of the week. God's wise and loving nature might not decide all the details of his will, since sometimes various alternative actions may equally well express his wisdom and love. So some details might be decided by his arbitrary will or choice or whim. But this is hardly objectionable (see Carson 2012: 445, 458–63).

(Trivializing God's goodness, §2.3) What does it mean to say "What God does is good"? Doesn't DCT trivialize it by reducing it to "What God does accords with his desires"? Even hateful people can follow their desires.

"What God does is good" means "What God does is desired by the highest available wisdom and love." This doesn't trivialize God's goodness. If God were hateful, then something else would be the highest available wisdom and love – and this something else would judge God harshly, as "not good." So our definition of "good action" doesn't make it true by definition that God's actions (even if hateful) are good.

(Sovereignty argument, §2.4) We previously mentioned and criticized the sovereignty argument for DCT. Does moving to our modified DCT change anything here?

Some may object that our modified DCT limits God's moral sovereignty, since it requires that God be wise and loving in order to create the moral law. But God is morally sovereign *because he's supremely wise and loving*.

Aren't we then judging God by human standards of wisdom and love? We have to do this to distinguish between God (who is qualified to create the moral law) and Ares (who isn't). Our descriptions of wisdom and love are only minimal standards that a Creator must pass in order to create the moral law, standards that God supremely passes but Ares fails. God's wisdom and love far surpass our human descriptions.

(Biblical argument, §2.4) We mentioned and criticized the biblical argument for DCT. Does moving to our modified DCT change anything here?

Our modified DCT is compatible with the Bible and may lead us, when we read the Bible, to emphasize God's wisdom and love, and to see God's desires as growing out of these.

(Circularity problem, §2.5) Does our modified DCT have any problem with circularity?

When we sketched analyses of "wise" and "loving" (§§3.2–3.3), we explained various ways to avoid circularity. And we presented much of our modified DCT in terms of "Creator" instead of "God," since the latter may, as many use the term, have "good" built into its meaning.

(Atheism problem, §§2.5, 2.7.1, 3.4) If we define "good action" in terms of divine commands, then aren't we making it impossible for atheists to accept morality?

On our modified DCT, good action = action desired by the highest available wisdom and love. Atheists can accept this and add that, since there's no God, the highest available wisdom and love = human wisdom and love. They'd conclude that good action = action desired by human wisdom and love. So our modified DCT makes it possible for atheists to accept morality. However, we also pointed out some difficulties that arise from basing morality on human wisdom and love.

(Semantic problem, §§2.5, 3.6) DCT faces a dilemma: defining "good action" in terms of God's will leads to major problems, while common alternative approaches to the meaning of "good action" (empirical, emotivist, and non-naturalistic) are uncongenial to DCT.

On our modified DCT, "good action" means "action desired by the highest available wisdom and love." This avoids problems with defining "good" directly using God's will and with combining DCT with other views on the meaning of "good."

(Knowing God's will, §2.6) We suggested that the traditional DCT can adequately explain how we can know God's will. Does moving to our modified DCT change anything?

Our modified DCT emphasizes *wisdom and love*. And so these would be more important in coming to know God's will – and in countering crazy religious fanatics who think that actions like terrorism or persecution are God's will.

When our view speaks of the "highest *available* wisdom and love," does this mean highest *existing* wisdom and love, or highest wisdom and love that's *available* (*knowable*) to us? I'd say that the highest *existing* wisdom and love defines what *is* good and right, but applying this requires that this wisdom and love be somewhat *accessible* to us (and so we've argued that God's will is to some extent knowable to us, through a combination of the Bible, the church, prayer, and reason).

(Bigotry problem, §2.7.3) Some object that religious DCT ethics leads to narrow-mindedness and bigotry instead of thinking for ourselves about moral issues in a responsible and loving way. We replied that religious ethics needn't go that way – and that we'd do better to see God as giving us general norms and desiring that we use our minds to apply these as wisely and lovingly as we can. Does our modified DCT change anything here?

The emphasis on wisdom and love strengthens the response. It encourages us to see God's norms as flowing from his wisdom and love (instead of being arbitrary) and to use our minds to apply these norms as wisely and lovingly as we can.

You've avoided an issue that comes up in DCT discussions. Assume that God is loving. Is God loving out of *necessity* (not out of free will) – so he couldn't act in a hateful way? Or is God loving out of *free will* (not out of necessity) – so he could decide to act in a hateful way but doesn't?

This is a good question. I don't know the answer, sorry.[21]

3.9 Independent Duties

As we construct a religious moral philosophy, a central issue is whether or not *strong moral realism* is true:

Strong moral realism holds that there are moral facts about the value of actions (including oughtness, permissibility, and goodness) that hold independently of actual or hypothetical facts about will (desires, commands, approvals, and so on), including divine and human will.[22]

DCT says no to this (since God's will creates the moral order), while natural law says yes (so God clarifies the moral order but his will doesn't create it).

---

[21] For discussions on this, see Adams (1999: 46–49) and Kaye (2003).

[22] I use "*strong* moral realism" here because philosophers use "moral realism" in different ways, and some see DCT as a moral realism (Carson 2012: 467).

Since this strong moral realism issue is so controversial and difficult to resolve, I've tried to develop both approaches as strongly as possible: a modified DCT in this chapter and an independent-duties theory in the next three chapters.[23]

My sympathies favor strong moral realism and independent duties – perhaps because I tend to trust commonsense philosophical views. Here I'll give three reasons for preferring independent duties over modified DCT.

(1) How our modified DCT is set up presupposes a prior belief in the value of wisdom and love. Without such a prior belief, why would we affirm that moral authority depends on wisdom and love? The value of wisdom and love can't depend without circularity on other things (like divine or human desires, moral language, or pragmatic factors), since such justifications are discredited if they're unwise (e.g., inconsistent or based on falsehoods) or unloving (e.g., lead to cruelty). Modified DCT assumes the *value* of wisdom and love but can't make this depend on other factors; so it seems to assume, inconsistently, a strong moral realism about the *independent* value of wisdom and love.

(2) Why is one account of wisdom and love *better* than another? What makes "Have concern for your friends but hate your enemies" an *incorrect analysis* of the sense of "loving" central to moral rationality? And what makes a theory of moral rationality *correct*? I can't see how this could be adequately based on divine or human desires, moral language, or pragmatic considerations. In defending a view of moral rationality, we can't appeal to *actual desires* (since these could be unwise or unloving) or *hypothetical idealized desires* (since the issue is how to specify the idealization). So how could one account of moral rationality be *objectively better* than another if strong moral realism isn't true?

(3) Consider this analogue of the *Euthyphro* question:

> Are wisdom and love good because the
> highest available wisdom and love supports them?
> Or do wisdom and love have independent value?

Modified DCT has to take the first alternative: *Wisdom and love are good because the highest available wisdom and love supports them.* This

---

[23] I partly follow Carson on this. He says (Carson 2000: 215) that questions about *axiological realism* (a cousin of my "strong moral realism") "are extremely difficult and perplexing; the issue may not be rationally decidable at the present state of philosophical discussion." His sympathies are *against* strong moral realism, and so he develops a modified DCT. My sympathies, however, are *in favor of* strong moral realism.

is circular – beings that are wise and loving would likely desire that others be wise and loving too – but why care about this unless we already believe in the value of wisdom and love? The objective-duties view affirms that *wisdom and love have independent value* (both in themselves and as a way to discover other moral values) and that this doesn't come from a verbal stipulation or anything of this sort.

While I favor independent duties over DCT, both views share much and can learn from each other. While both can emphasize wisdom, love, and following God's will, they differ on whether wisdom and love have an independent, objective value. Both views are similar in practice; but their theoretical bases differ.

PART II

ETHICS AS NATURAL LAWS

4

Natural Law and Rationality

Most religious thinkers accept duties independent of God's will. Rejecting DCT, they don't think that hatred is wrong because God forbids it (or even because a wise and loving God forbids it); instead, God forbids hatred because he knows that it's already wrong (and wrong in itself). While ethics and religion connect in many ways, they're also somewhat independent; so ethics doesn't presume religion or belief in God.

These next three chapters explore how this might work, using some ideas from natural law. This chapter (*rationality*) is about practical reason. The next (*biology*) is about our biological nature and what norms this leads to using practical reason. The third (*spirituality*) is about our relationship to God.

4.1 Natural Law

The term "natural law" (NL) refers both to *moral principles*, understood in a certain way, and to an *ethical tradition*, whose central focus is St. Thomas Aquinas (1224–74).

(1) "Natural law" refers to objective *moral principles* that are "written on the human heart" (as opposed to coming from society or revelation). Such norms are instinctive or based on ordinary reasoning. They're the same for everyone, authoritative over our actions, and known by virtually everyone.

Aquinas saw NL as part of how God uses laws to govern the world. He defined "law" as an "ordinance of reason for the common good, made by him who has care over the community, and promulgated." He distinguished several types of law:

- *Eternal law* includes physical laws, moral laws, and revealed religious laws.
- *Natural law* (moral law) is that part of the eternal law that can be known by our natural reason and that applies to our free-will choices.
- *Biblical law* is law revealed through the Bible, to supplement and reinforce NL and to guide us to our supernatural goal of eternal happiness with God.
- *Human law* is civil law created by human societies to apply NL to particular circumstances; human rules that violate NL are considered, not unjust laws, but rather not laws at all.

Aquinas's central theme is the harmony between human reason and Christian faith. His ethics has two levels: *moral philosophy* is based on human reason and *moral theology* builds on this but also incorporates faith. Faith adds further duties and a broader context for ethics; so from faith we see that what ultimately makes an action bad is that it moves us away from our ultimate goal, which is complete happiness with God.

(2) "Natural law" also refers to an *ethical tradition* that sees moral norms (natural laws) as objective, based on nature instead of convention, and knowable to virtually everyone through natural human reason. Aquinas is the central figure. Many see the tradition as starting with Aristotle (384–322 BC), whose *Rhetoric* considered a natural justice binding on everyone, and the ancient Stoics, who believed in a natural moral law to be just toward everyone. Other major figures include Augustine (354–430); various medievals; Francisco Suárez (1548–1617), a Spanish Jesuit who opposed Spanish colonization as violating the natural rights of sovereign peoples; Hugo Grotius (1583–1645), who endorsed natural rights and international law; Samuel Pufendorf (1632–94), who systematized duties to God, self, and others; John Locke (1632–1704) and Joseph Butler (1692–1752), who criticized Thomas Hobbes's view that humans are by nature amoral egoists; and, more recently, Elizabeth Anscombe, John Finnis, Peter Geach, Germain Grisez, Anthony Kenny, Jacques Maritain, Alasdair MacIntyre, and Mark Murphy.[1]

---

[1] For introductions to natural law, see Aquinas (1274), Murphy (2011), and Finnis (2011). Also helpful are Haldane (1989) on medieval controversies and Madigan (2005: 561–65) on recent trends.

NL thinkers almost all support the golden rule (GR). Reiner (1983: 272–73) shows how Christians from early times connected the moral law that Paul saw written on everyone's heart (Romans 2:13–15), the Stoic natural moral law (built into everyone's reason), and the gospel GR that summed up the Law and the prophets (Matthew 7:12). Christians who saw GR as NL's core include Justin Martyr, Basil, Augustine, Gratian, Anselm, William of Champeaux, Peter Lombard, Hugh of St. Victor, John of Salisbury, Bonaventure, Scotus, Luther, Calvin, and Erasmus.[2] Aquinas (1274: I–II, q. 94, a. 4 & q. 99, a. 1), while emphasizing "Do good and avoid evil" more, saw GR as part of both natural and biblical law, and as analyzing "Love your neighbor as yourself" (loving X as myself = treating X as I want to be treated). Recent NL thinkers highlight GR; Finnis (2011: 420) writes, "To violate the golden rule is to allow emotional motivations for self-interested preference to override the rational rule of fair impartiality," and Grisez (2011: 232) suggests that we decide government's role in health care for poor people "by considering available resources and competing needs, and applying the golden rule." And a recent Vatican (2009) NL study emphasizes GR. GR is central to my view.

While NL views can be diverse, I take mainstream NL to accept God and strong moral realism and to reject DCT.[3]

This chapter and the next two construct an independent-duties NL approach to religious ethics. I'll develop four NL ideas:

- Practical reason and GR are the heart of moral thinking.
- Our duties depend on our nature, as rational-biological-spiritual beings. We can know our duties by combining practical reason (based on self-evident truths) with observation of human nature. While general moral norms are known to virtually everyone, specific duties can be less clear.
- Moral norms from reason largely overlap with biblical norms from revelation.
- Morality plays a key role in God's plan to lead us to eternal happiness with him, which is our final goal and fulfillment.

---

[2] See Wattles (1996: 69, 72, 208–9), du Roy (2008, 2009), and Pennington (2008).
[3] Things are less clear historically. Samuel Pufendorf and John Locke, who are often given as NL thinkers, also accepted DCT (see §§2.7.4–5).

My quirky NL view doesn't depict what Aquinas really meant; instead, it develops a broadly similar view adapted to modern thinking (including evolution). As Chapter 3 tried to construct the strongest possible modified DCT, so also Chapters 4–6 try to construct the strongest possible independent-duties NL view.

4.2 Practical Reason

The *supreme practical-reason principle* (RAT, for "rationality") is fairly simple. I give two formulations. The first is an "ought" that applies to all rational beings, but with qualifications:

RAT: As rational beings decide how to act on important matters (and as they form related desires or moral beliefs), they ought as far as practically possible to be vividly aware of the relevant facts, avoid falsehoods, and be consistent.

RAT's second formulation is a *simplified imperative form*:

RAT: Be vividly aware of the facts, avoid falsehoods, and be consistent.

I'll move freely between the two forms (with the technical form's qualifications being implicit in the simpler form). I'll now add nine points to clarify RAT.

(1) If you disdainfully say, "Of course this is true, this is just common sense," then I'll be happy. I see RAT as the basic self-evident principle of NL that's "written on the human heart" – objective, the same for everyone, prescriptively authoritative over all our actions, known by virtually everyone through natural reason, assumed by virtually every approach to ethics – *and* an independent duty in the strong moral-realism sense. It's ordinary but *not* trivial; we can extract from it a useful way of thinking about moral choices that's much in harmony with the natural-law GR tradition.

(2) When applied to frail, finite beings like ourselves, RAT needs a slew of qualifications ("as we decide how to act *on important matters, . . . as far as practically possible, . . .* aware of the *relevant facts*" – and likely others are needed too). We humans are limited in our ability to know the facts, be vividly aware of them, avoid falsehoods, and be consistent. When applied to an infinite rational being (God), RAT can be expressed more simply: "*Be vividly aware of every fact, accept no falsehoods, and be completely consistent in every way.*" Humans can only strive to mirror imperfectly an ideal of practical rationality that God fulfills completely.

We are rational beings, yes, in the weak sense of having certain rational capacities that RAT presupposes; for example, we can form beliefs, imagine situations vividly, avoid falsehoods, and recognize inconsistencies. We do these only better or worse, never perfectly. We base our actions, desires, and moral beliefs on a greater or lesser grasp of the facts, a greater or lesser vividness of imagination, a greater or lesser avoidance of error, and a greater or lesser consistency. And so our practical rationality can be greater or lesser. Other things being equal, our actions, desires, and moral beliefs are more rational to the extent that they're more informed, imaginative, and consistent.

The qualified form says "aware of the *relevant* facts." Very roughly, a fact is *more relevant* to our decision (or desire or moral belief) if it would or should make a *larger difference* to our decision. Since we're often limited by time constraints, we should, other things equal, give priority to getting those facts that would make a bigger difference to our decision.[4]

(3) RAT applies to us humans because we're *rational beings* (again, in the weak sense of having certain rational capacities). RAT would also apply if we were another kind of rational being, perhaps Martians. The next chapter will consider moral norms that apply to us because we're *human*, with peculiarities that distinguish humans, not only from other animals, but also from other imaginable rational beings.

(4) RAT, which says "be aware of the facts" and "avoid falsehoods," echoes a point made by William James (1896: 17):

> We must know the truth, and we must avoid error – these are our first and great commandments as would-be knowers; but they are not two ways of stating an identical commandment, they are two separable laws.

We can be too skeptical (overstressing "Avoid error," at the cost of losing much truth) or too gullible (overstressing "Know the truth," at the cost of accepting much error). We need to fulfill both commandments, as well as we can, in a balanced way – both as knowers and as agents. While James and I both recognize these two commandments, neither of us has a neat formula for how to achieve this balance. We shouldn't demand too much precision in RAT – which is rough but indispensable.

James's commandments and mine require an "on important matters" qualification. As knowers, we have no duty to add *trivial* true beliefs (like

---

[4] This is useful but rough. See Carson (2012) for problems in precisely defining what facts are "relevant to" a decision (or desire or moral belief).

"My bathroom has 8,631 tiles"). As agents, we need to invest energy on matters of some importance (like how to treat my neighbor and not which finger to use to scratch my ear). I'm unsure how to measure "importance"; a rough suggestion is that we look at how our beliefs and actions affect desires (including desires to know our place in the universe and desires of other people on how they're to be treated).

(5) RAT is to be taken in a *nonnaturalistic* and *strongly realistic* way, as objective, true by virtue of independent moral facts, and not reducible to descriptive, empirical, or emotional terms. I see RAT and other ought-judgments as *objective prescriptions* (objective truths that logically entail imperatives for action and commit us to acting accordingly under penalty of inconsistency) and thus as authoritative for rational agents.[5]

RAT is a *self-evident truth*. This means that RAT under favorable conditions can be known to be true without being based on any further argument or justification. The ideas behind RAT (but not the exact wording) are presupposed by almost everyone working in the field of ethics. Most will see RAT as obviously true; and extended investigation would reveal no absurd implications. In the colorful language of traditional NL, RAT is "written on the human heart." In the colorful language of modern evolution, RAT is "hard-coded into our genes."

Besides the very abstract RAT, my view needn't accept any other basic norms as self-evident. This distinguishes my view from nonnaturalisms like those of G. E. Moore (1903) and C. D. Ross (1930), who take as self-evident substantive and often controversial norms (such as utilitarianism for Moore and a nonutilitarian promise-keeping duty for Ross). So my view avoids the big objection to nonnaturalism: that it rests on vague and variable moral intuitions.

RAT cannot be defended without circularity. Any argument assumes the value of truth (in premises and conclusion) and consistency (valid reasoning constrains us because accepting the premises forces us under pain of inconsistency to accept the conclusion). Instead of resting on

---

[5] J. L. Mackie (1977: 23, 31) sees this understanding of "ought" as part of our philosophical tradition, our ordinary thinking, and our moral language: "The main tradition of European moral philosophy from Plato onwards has combined the view that moral values are objective with the recognition that moral judgments are partly prescriptive or directive or action-guiding.... This objectivism about values... has also a firm basis in ordinary thought, and even in the meanings of moral terms." While Mackie rejects the idea, I accept it, as does John Hare (2001: 20): "This idea of objective prescriptivity is the center of my own view, what I call prescriptive realism. The difference between Mackie and me is that he thinks this is an error and I think it is the truth."

further reasoning, RAT is a basic presupposition of reason and the first duty of a rational being.

(6) While RAT is the basic practical-reason axiom, we'll later mention subsidiary practical-reason norms that apply to us in terms of our social and emotional nature (§5.2.4). We can argue for subsidiary norms by looking for what further practical-reason norms we'd endorse for humans insofar as we followed RAT. These subsidiary norms also form part of what constitutes practical wisdom for humans.[6]

(7) RAT can also be expressed in terms of *virtues* (good character traits), as analyzing what Aristotle called the intellectual virtue of *practical wisdom*:

> RAT: To have the virtue of *practical wisdom* is to be disposed, as we decide how to act on important matters (and form related desires or moral beliefs), to be vividly aware of the relevant facts, avoid falsehoods, be consistent, and satisfy subsidiary practical-reason norms for humans.

Subvirtues of *practical wisdom* include things like *being informed*, *being imaginative (empathetic)*, and *being consistent*.

God's wisdom includes satisfying RAT (knowing everything in a vivid way, having no false beliefs, and being entirely consistent). It may also include other things; if God has emotions, then his wisdom likely includes things mentioned in §5.2.4, like a passion for the truth, a hatred of falsehoods (including false stereotypes), and deep feelings of concern for people.

(8) RAT may seem to be more about reason in general than about *practical* reason. But two elements relate it in a special way to practice. First, *vivid awareness* is needed to appreciate the experienced impact of actions on myself and others; so if my smoking may bring lung cancer, then, in deciding whether to smoke, I need to be *vividly aware* of what having lung cancer would be like. Second, "consistency" is used in a broader way to apply to important areas of practical reason. RAT, since it's so close to key elements of *theoretical reason*, is difficult to reject. Should we reject the general importance of gaining truth, avoiding falsehood, and being consistent? This is intellectual suicide and would harm science and math.

---

[6] Gensler (2011a: 96) says, "We're rational in our moral judgments to the extent that we're consistent, informed, imaginative, and a few more things." Here "informed" = RAT's "be aware of the facts and avoid falsehoods"; "imaginative" = RAT's "*vividly* aware"; and "a few more things" = RAT's "subsidiary norms of practical reason" (see Gensler 2011a: 98; 1996: 151–52).

Or should we reject RAT's extensions (*vivid awareness* and *consistency applied to practical reason*)? Why do that?

(9) RAT leads to GR (we'll do details later): "Be vividly aware of the relevant facts (especially about how your action affects another and what it would be like to be treated that way yourself), avoid falsehoods (about this), and be consistent (so don't treat another as you're unwilling that you be treated in the same situation)."

4.3 Consistency

RAT's consistency part can be expressed as follows (I'll mostly use the simpler form):

- *Technical*: As rational beings decide how to act on important matters (and as they form related desires or moral beliefs), they ought as far as practically possible to be consistent.
- *Simplified*: Be consistent.

RAT prescribes consistency, not only in beliefs, but also in further areas of practical reason: consistency of will, conscientiousness, impartiality, and the golden rule. Consistency is the basis for key elements of practical reason, including reflective equilibrium, ends-means rationality, and the golden rule. Consistency doesn't tell us exactly what to think or do; instead, it forbids combinations that don't fit together.[7]

(1) *Consistency in beliefs* tells us not to accept logically incompatible beliefs – and not to accept a belief without also accepting its logical consequences.

I've had a beard on and off for much of my life. I sometimes meet people who say things like "All bearded people are crazy." I like to challenge their consistency. So I ask, "Did Jesus Christ and Abraham Lincoln have beards?" They say yes. I ask, "Were they crazy?" They say no. Then I say, "You contradicted yourself." These three statements form a logically inconsistent set:

- All bearded people are crazy.
- Jesus and Lincoln are bearded people.
- Jesus and Lincoln aren't crazy.

---

[7] Consistency duties have implicit qualifications (Gensler 1996: 19–23), for example, for cases when we *can't be consistent* (perhaps because of emotional turmoil or the inability to grasp complex logical relationships) or where being consistent in a minor way *has very bad results* (maybe migraine headaches); in practice, these qualifications aren't very important. For more on consistency, see Gensler (1996, 2010, 2013).

So consistency forbids combining all three at once:

- I believe "All bearded people are crazy."
- I believe "Jesus and Lincoln are bearded people."
- I believe "Jesus and Lincoln aren't crazy."

Consistency doesn't tell you specifically what to believe. It just forbids a combination; so if you accept all three then you have to give up at least one.

Or suppose that, after drinking too much, you believe that all humans are grasshoppers and that the pope is human, but you don't believe that the pope is a grasshopper. Then you violate consistency, which forbids this combination:

- I believe "All humans are grasshoppers."
- I believe "The pope is human."
- I don't believe "The pope is a grasshopper."

There are two reasons not to combine these: (1) the three are inconsistent and (2) you shouldn't believe that all humans are grasshoppers (and so you shouldn't combine believing this with believing other things). Note that our consistency norm doesn't tell you to accept the conclusion that the pope is a grasshopper; it just forbids a combination.

Consistency pushes us toward a *reflective equilibrium* in our thinking between principles and concrete judgments. Suppose I accept an appealing moral principle but reject an unappealing concrete judgment that it logically entails. Then something has to give; I have to reject the principle or accept the concrete judgment. Before deciding which to do, I need to investigate the principle further. Much moral thinking follows this reflective-equilibrium pattern, which appeals to consistency.

(2) *Consistency of will* tells us, for example, not to have incompatible all-things-considered desires – not to have resolutions that conflict with actions – and not to combine having an end, believing that achieving this end requires carrying out certain means, and not carrying out the means.

Consistency forbids this combination:

- I resolve to eat nothing.
- I eat this granola bar.

If I do both, then I'm inconsistent and I have a consistency duty to change something; but consistency alone doesn't tell me what to do, since that depends on the situation. If my medical exam requires fasting, then I should presumably do the resolving and avoid the eating. But if my fasting is an unhealthy way to diet, then I should presumably eat and avoid the resolving.

Consistency requires a harmony between ends and means. Suppose that Maria wants to become a doctor. She realizes that, to do this, she needs to study hard. But she doesn't act accordingly. Ends-means consistency forbids this combination:

- I have the goal of becoming a doctor.
- I believe that achieving this goal requires that I study hard.
- I don't study hard.

Since Maria's goals, beliefs, and actions don't fit together, she must change something. Maybe her doctor-goal is unrealistic and should be rejected; or maybe she just needs to carry out the means. Consistency doesn't say what to change.

Some goals are evil. Our ends-means imperatives don't command evil means to promote an evil goal; instead, they just forbid a combination, like this one:

- I have the goal to get maximal revenge against Victoria.
- I believe that achieving this goal requires that I delete the sole copy of her dissertation.
- I don't delete the sole copy of her dissertation.

You shouldn't combine these, because (1) the three are inconsistent and (2) you shouldn't have this goal (and so you shouldn't combine having this goal with doing other things). Consistency just forbids a combination; it doesn't say that, if you in fact happen to have this goal and this belief, then you ought to do the act. So ends-means consistency won't prescribe evil actions, even if we have evil goals.

Ends and means are important to practical reason and human life. We have many goals – including food, shelter, health, companionship, meaningfulness, and eternal life. Practical reason has us try to understand our goals, investigate how to satisfy them, satisfy ends-means consistency, and reject ends or means that lead us to violate golden-rule consistency.

(3) *Conscientiousness* tells us to keep our actions, resolutions, and desires in harmony with our moral beliefs. Suppose I believe that *one ought never to kill a human being for any reason*. If I'm conscientious, then I'll never intentionally kill a human being, I'll resolve not to kill for any reason (even to protect myself or my family), and I won't want others to kill for any reason. Similar requirements cover beliefs about what is "all right" ("permissible"). If I'm conscientious, then I won't do

something without believing that it would be *all right* for me to do. And I won't believe that something is *all right* without consenting to the idea of it being done.[8]

Conscientiousness can be a tool for criticizing moral beliefs. Suppose I was taught to discriminate against short people and to believe *shortism*: "All short people ought to be beat up, just because they're short." Now shortism entails "If I were short, then I ought to be beat up"; so consistency in beliefs commits me to accepting this too. But then, by conscientiousness, I'm committed to *desiring that if I were short then I be beat up*. So then consistency forbids this combination:

- I *believe* "All short people ought to be beat up, just because they're short."
- I don't *desire* that if I were short, then I be beat up.

When I understand short people (including how it feels for them to be beat up) and how my negative attitudes about them originated (through social indoctrination), and I vividly imagine myself being beaten up in their place, then I likely *won't* desire that if I were short then I be beat up. But then I'm inconsistent in accepting shortism.

(4) *Impartiality* tells us to make similar evaluations about similar actions, regardless of the individuals involved. Impartiality requires that our beliefs be consistent with universalizability (Gensler 2010: 285–87):

Universalizability: Whatever is right (wrong, good, bad, and so on) in one case would also be right (wrong, good, bad, and so on) in any exactly or relevantly similar case, regardless of the individuals involved.

If I'm impartial, then I'll evaluate an act based on what it's like – and not based on who plays what role in the situation; I'll apply the same standards to myself that I apply to others. I violate impartiality if I make conflicting evaluations about acts that I regard as *exactly similar* or *relevantly similar*.[9]

---

[8] Such conscientiousness principles require that key terms be taken in certain ways (for example, that "ought" be used in an all-things-considered, evaluative sense). Gensler (2013: 31–33) has more details.

[9] Two actions are *exactly similar* if they have all the same *universal properties* in common. Here a *universal property* is a nonevaluative property describable without proper names (like "Gensler" or "Chicago") or pointer terms (like "I" or "this"); an *exactly reversed* situation switches all the universal properties of the action (see Gensler 1996: 69–92; 2010: 324–25; 2013: 33). In this context, take "properties" to mean "universal properties."

Here's a Good Samaritan example (Luke 10:30–35). Suppose that, while jogging, I see a man who's been beaten, robbed, and left to die. Should I help him, perhaps by making a phone call? I think of excuses why I shouldn't; I'm busy and don't want to get involved. I say, "It would be all right for me not to help him." But then I consider an exactly similar reversed situation, where our properties are switched. I imagine myself in *his* exact place; so I'm the one who's been beaten, robbed, and left to die. And I imagine him in *my* exact place; so he's jogging and sees me in my sad state. I ask myself, "Would it be all right for this man not to help me in this reversed situation? Surely not!" But then I'm inconsistent, since I accept this combination:

- I believe "It's all right for me not to help this person."
- I believe "If the situation were exactly reversed, then it would be wrong for this person not to help me."

What's all right for me to do to another must be all right for the other to do to me in an imagined exactly similar situation.

In the actual world, no two acts are exactly similar. But I can always *imagine* an exactly similar act. If I'm about to do something to another, to test my impartiality, I can *imagine* what it would be like for this to be done to me in an exactly similar situation. Consistency forbids this combination:

- I believe "It's right for me to do A to another."
- I believe "It's wrong for A to be done to me in the same situation."

In the imagined "same situation," I switch in my mind the properties of myself and the other person. So if I'm ABC and the other person is XYZ, then I imagine myself being XYZ and the other person being ABC.[10]

My example uses an *imagined* second case. But we can use an *actual* second case, if there's one handy. Suppose I cut X off in traffic and I think this is right. Later, Y cuts me off and I think this is wrong. But I ask, "Why would cutting-someone-off be right for me to do but wrong for another to do?" Since I find no reason, I conclude that the

---

[10] Instead of switching *every* property in my mind, I could switch just those relevant to evaluating the act. If I'm unsure whether a property is relevant, I could switch it anyway – just to be safe.

two acts are *relevantly similar*.[11] But then my combination of beliefs is inconsistent:

- I believe "It's right for me to cut X off."
- I believe "It's wrong for Y to cut me off."
- I believe "These two acts are relevantly similar."

I violate impartiality, since my three beliefs don't fit together. I must reject at least one belief. I could hold that both actions are wrong, or that both are right, or that one act was right but not the other because of such and such differences. So, while impartiality doesn't say specifically what to believe, it guides me on how to work out my beliefs in a consistent way.

In deciding whether two actions are *relevantly similar*, we appeal to antecedent moral beliefs about which factors give reasons for a given moral appraisal. Impartiality pushes us to apply these reasons in the same way to our actions and to another's actions. But it's often cleaner to appeal to *imagined exactly similar actions* – and so I'll emphasize these.

Impartiality here is about *evaluating similar cases similarly*. It doesn't say to treat everyone the same, regardless of how they relate to us. I can consistently judge that I ought to have greater concern for my children so long as I judge that in similar cases other parents ought to have greater concern for their children.

(5) *The golden rule* forbids this combination:

- I do A to another.
- I'm unwilling that A be done to me in the same situation.[12]

GR is so important that it deserves its own section.

---

[11] Two actions are *relevantly similar* if the reasons why one fits in a given moral category (good, bad, right, wrong, or whatever) also apply to the other; here "reasons" are universal properties relevant to the morality of the action.

[12] "Unwilling" here can be taken as "objecting to." Then the forbidden combination is (1) I do A to another and (2) I object to the idea of A being done to me in the same situation. If we're playing chess, I object to the idea of your cheating to beat me (I'm unwilling that you do this), but I don't object to the idea of your beating me if you do so fairly (I'm in this sense "willing" that you do this). (I thank Tom Carson for this clarification and example.)

4.4 Golden Rule

The golden rule says "Treat others as you want to be treated."[13] GR is a global standard, endorsed by nearly every religion and culture, important for families and professionals across the planet, and a key part of a growing global-ethics movement.

I like to use this story to introduce GR.[14] There once was a grandpa who lived with his family. As Grandpa grew older, he began to slobber and spill his food; so the family had him eat alone. When he dropped his bowl and broke it, they scolded him and got him a cheap wooden bowl. Grandpa was so unhappy. Now one day the young grandson was working with wood. "What are you doing?" Mom and Dad asked. "I'm making a wooden bowl," he said, "for when you two get old and must eat alone." Mom and Dad then looked sad and realized how they were mistreating Grandpa. So they decided to keep quiet when he spills his food and to let him eat with the family.

The heart of the golden rule is *switching places*. You step into another's shoes. What you do to Grandpa, you imagine being done to you. You ask, "Am I willing that if I were in the same situation then I be treated that same way?"

The golden rule seems simple. But the usual wording is loose and invites objections; many academics dismiss GR as a folksy proverb that self-destructs when analyzed carefully. I think we just need to understand GR more clearly.

I put my attempt at a clearer wording on a shirt.[15] It has "the golden rule" surrounded by symbols for eight GR religions (Bahá'í, Buddhism, Christianity, Confucianism, Hinduism, Islam, Judaism, and Taoism). It also has my GR formula:

> Treat others only as you consent to
> being treated in the same situation.

My formula is intended to help us apply GR to difficult cases.

---

[13] For more on GR, see Gensler (2013, 2014), R. M. Hare (1963), Wattles (1996), Shapiro (2015), and the other Gensler entries in the bibliography.

[14] My story is "The old man and his grandson" (Grimm Brothers 1812). Variations exist across the globe, including a Buddhist version from ancient India (http://www.sacred-texts.com/bud/j4/j4010.htm, search for "murder").

[15] You can get your own GR shirt, in many styles and colors, from my GR web page (http://www.harryhiker.com/gr). This popular page also has GR information, videos, stories, chronology, links, and so on.

My GR formula commands consistency. It demands a fit between my act toward another and my desire about how I'd be treated in the same situation. It doesn't replace other moral norms or theories or give all the answers. It doesn't say specifically what to do (so it doesn't command bad actions if we have flawed desires); instead, it forbids an inconsistent combination:

- I do A to another.
- I'm unwilling that A be done to me in the same situation.

GR, far from being vague, is a precise consistency test. Suppose I force Grandpa to eat alone. I switch places in my mind: I imagine that *I* am forced to eat alone in the same situation. Do I condemn this same act done to me? Then I condemn how I treat Grandpa. *I condemn how I treat another if I condemn the same act when I imagine it done to me in the same situation.*

People who reject GR usually understand it crudely, often as:

Literal GR: If you want X to do A to you, then do A to X.

The literal GR has no same-situation clause and it commands a specific act (instead of forbidding an inconsistent combination). This literal GR often works well. Suppose you want Lucy to be kind to you; then you're to be kind to her. Or suppose you want Adam not to hurt you (or rob you, or be rude to you); then you aren't to do these things to him. These applications seem sensible. But the literal GR can lead to absurdities in two ways.

First, you may be in a *different situation* from the other person. Consider this instance of the literal GR:

Suppose your father is hard of hearing: if you want your father not to speak more loudly to you (since your hearing is normal), then don't speak more loudly to him.

This ignores differences between you and your father. To get around this problem, you need a same-situation qualifier: "How do I desire that I'd be treated *if I were in the same situation as my father* (and thus hard of hearing)?" You desire that if you were in his same situation then people would speak loudly to you; so you speak loudly to him.

We can take "same" situation here as "exactly similar" or "relevantly similar." In the first case, I imagine myself in my father's *exact place* (with all his properties). In the second, I imagine myself having those properties of my father (such as being hard of hearing) that I think are or might be *relevant* to deciding how to speak to him. Either approach works fine.

Here's another case where the literal GR leads to problems:

To a patient: if you want the doctor to remove your appendix, then remove the doctor's appendix.

Again, we need a same-situation qualifier. The patient clearly doesn't desire that if he were in the place of his doctor (with a healthy appendix), then his appendix be removed by a sick patient ignorant of medicine. As you apply GR, ask this question:

> Am I now <u>willing that if</u> I were in the same
> situation then this be done to me?

The other person's situation includes likes and dislikes. So if you're a waiter who hates broccoli, but your customer likes and orders it, then you imagine being served broccoli in a hypothetical situation where you like and order it.

Here's yet another instance of the literal GR:

To a parent: if you want your child not to punish you, then don't punish him.

Again, we need a same-situation clause. Suppose that I have a two-year-old son, Willie, who puts fingers into electrical outlets. I try to discourage him from doing this, but nothing works. Finally, I decide that I need to punish him when he does it. I want to see if I can punish him without violating GR. I should ask this question:

> Am I now <u>willing that if</u> I were in the same
> situation as Willie then I be punished?

I'd answer yes (since punishment would likely have saved my life). I might add, "I'm thankful that my parents punished me in such cases, even though I wasn't pleased then." So here I can punish my child without breaking GR, since I'm willing that if I were in the same situation then I be treated the same way.

People often ask the GR question wrongly, which forces them to do whatever the other person wants. They ask, "If I were in the other person's place, how would I then want to be treated?" Now if you were in little Willie's place (not knowing about electricity and not wanting to be punished for playing with outlets), then you wouldn't want to be punished. If we misapply GR, we'd conclude that we shouldn't punish Willie for putting his fingers into outlets. So it's better to apply GR as explained earlier. I can punish little Willie (to save his life), since I'm now willing that if I were in his situation then I be punished. In asking the GR question, it's important to say "willing that if":

> Am I now willing that if I were in the same
> situation then this be done to me?

Immanuel Kant's (1785: 97) objection to GR rests on this confusion. Here you're a judge, about to sentence a dangerous criminal to jail. The criminal protests and appeals (incorrectly) to GR: "If you were in my place, you wouldn't want to be sent to jail; so by the golden rule you can't send me to jail." You should respond: "I can send you to jail, because I'm now willing that if I were in your place (as a dangerous criminal) then I be sent to jail." You could add, "If I do such things, then please send me to jail too!"

Sometimes we need to act against what others want. We may need to stop a baby who wants to put fingers into outlets, refuse a salesperson who wants to sell us overpriced products, fail a student who doesn't work, defend ourselves against an attacker, or jail a dangerous criminal. And yes, we're now willing that if we were in their situation then we be treated that way. GR lets us act against what others want, as long as we're now willing that if we were in their situation then we be treated similarly.

Recall that the literal GR can lead to absurdities in two ways. We dealt with the *different-circumstances* problem by adding a same-situation clause. A second problem is that the literal GR can tell us to do bad things if we have *flawed desires* about how we're to be treated. I'll give three examples.

There once was a woman named Electra. Electra wanted to follow GR, but she got her facts wrong; she thought electrical shocks were pleasant. Since she wanted others to shock her, she applied the literal GR and shocked them:

To Electra (who thinks electrical shocks are pleasant): if you want others to give you electrical shocks, then give them electrical shocks.

Given flawed desires, the literal GR can command evil actions.

We'll use a triple strategy for dealing with flawed desires.

(1) Emphasize that GR, instead of telling us specifically what to do, just forbids a combination:

- I give electrical shocks to another.
- I'm unwilling that electrical shocks be given to me in the same situation.

Since the consistency GR doesn't say specifically what to do, it doesn't tell Electra to do evil things (like shock others).

(2) Emphasize that GR consistency, to lead reliably to right action, needs to combine with other things, like knowledge and imagination. If we're misinformed, then we might do evil things without violating GR consistency. Here Electra shocks others (an evil thing) but satisfies GR consistency (she's willing that she be shocked in similar cases), since she's misinformed and thinks these shocks are pleasurable.

(3) Use reason against flawed desires. Here we'd show Electra that electrical shocks *are* painful (perhaps by giving her a small one). Once she understands this, GR consistency will lead her away from shocking others.

Here's another example. Mona hates herself and wants others to hate her; so, following the literal GR, she hates others. But again, (1) the correctly formulated GR just forbids a combination and so doesn't prescribe that she hate others and (2) GR consistency, to lead reliably to right action, has to combine with other things (like knowledge, imagination, and here *a healthy self-love*). Also, (3) we can use reason against Mona's flawed desires. We can try to help Mona understand *why* she hates herself and *how* to neutralize this hatred – by not fixating on her negatives but by seeing herself and her good points in a more balanced way, and, if she's a believer, by appreciating that God loves her. Once Mona regains a healthy self-love, GR consistency will lead her more readily to love others.

Or suppose Adolf is a Nazi who so hates Jews that he kills them and desires that he be killed if he were Jewish (or found to be Jewish). The literal GR would tell Adolph to kill Jews:

To Adolph (a Jew-hating Nazi): if you want others to kill you if you were Jewish, then kill others who are Jewish.

Again, we can make three points. (1) GR, properly formulated, doesn't command specific actions but instead just forbids an inconsistent combination:

- I kill others just because they're Jewish.
- I'm unwilling that if I were Jewish then I'd be killed just because I'm Jewish.

Since the consistency GR doesn't say specifically what to do, it doesn't tell Adolph to kill Jews. (2) GR consistency, to lead reliably to right action, has to combine with other things (like knowledge, imagination, and here *rational desires*). (3) We can use reason against Adoph's flawed desires. We can try to help him understand *why* he hates Jews so much, even desiring that he be killed if he were found out to be Jewish. His anti-Jewish hatred likely has its source in things that can be rationally criticized. Maybe Adolph thinks Aryans are superior to Jews and racially pure; we can criticize this on factual grounds. Or maybe Adolph was taught to hate Jews by his family and friends; maybe they hated Jews, called them names, and spread false stereotypes about them. And so his anti-Jewish desires likely came from false beliefs and social conditioning; such flawed desires would diminish if he understood their origin and broadened his experience and knowledge of Jews in an open and personal way. With greater rationality, Adolph wouldn't desire that he'd be killed if found out to be Jewish – and GR would be a powerful tool against his racism.

While this example was about a Nazi, the same idea applies to those who desire that they be mistreated if they were black, female, gay, or whatever. Such desires are likely flawed (as based on a social conditioning that uses false beliefs and stereotypes) and would be given up if we expanded our knowledge and experience of the group in an open and personal way.

As you apply the golden rule, keep in mind that it doesn't work alone. To lead reliably to right action, GR consistency needs to build on things like knowledge, imagination, creativity, rationalized desires, and a healthy self-love.

Why does consistency require the golden rule? Suppose I hit you but I'm unwilling that I be hit in the same situation. Why is that inconsistent?

GR rests on two consistency norms: that we be *impartial* (in the sense of making similar evaluations about similar actions, regardless of the individuals involved) and *conscientious* (in the sense of living in harmony with our moral beliefs). If I'm impartial and conscientiousness, then I'll necessarily follow GR:

> If I'm consistent, then I won't *hit* you unless I believe that it would be *all right* for me to hit you. (conscientiousness)
> If I'm consistent, then I won't believe that it would be all right for me to hit *you* unless I also believe that it would be all right for *me* to be hit in the same situation. (impartiality)
> If I'm consistent, then I won't believe that it would be *all right* for me to be hit in the same situation unless I'm also *willing* that I be hit in the same situation. (conscientiousness)
> ∴ If I'm consistent, then I won't hit you unless I'm also willing that I be hit in the same situation.

So this combination is inconsistent: (1) I do A to another and (2) I'm unwilling that A be done to me in the same situation.[16]

So my GR can be based on an abstract argument; similar reasoning justifies many variations. We can consider someone else we care about (maybe our daughter) on the receiving end of the action. We can give consistency conditions, not for *doing something*, but for *wanting something to be done* or for *holding a moral belief*. A *multiparty GR* has us satisfy GR toward each affected party. A *future-regard form* has us imagine ourselves suffering the future consequences of our present action. A *self-regard form* has us imagine someone we care about doing the self-destructive thing we're doing to ourselves. My *formula of universal law* is a generalized GR that contains many of these: "Act only as you're willing for anyone to act in the same situation, regardless of where or when you imagine yourself or others." GR can also be expressed as about virtue or rights:

- *Consideration for others* = being disposed to treat others only as we're willing to be treated in the same situation.
- Everyone has the *right* to be treated by others only as these others are willing to have themselves treated in the same circumstances.

GR can be, and historically has been, expressed in many ways. GR is a family of related ideas more than a single idea.

The golden rule fits many perspectives. Philosophically, GR could be a self-evident truth (or as derivable from such), God's will, a cultural convention, a social contract for mutual advantage, socially useful, reflecting our feelings, promoting self-interest (since it brings self-respect and better treatment from others), and so on. Religiously, GR is part of Bahá'í, Buddhism, Christianity, Confucianism, Hinduism, Islam, Judaism, Sikhism, Taoism, Zoroastrianism, and so on. Diverse groups share GR.[17] The golden rule can be a point of unity in a diverse world.

4.5 Knowledge and Imagination

RAT's nonconsistency part goes this way (again, I'll mostly use the simpler form and regard qualifications as implicit):

---

[16] My logic textbook (Gensler 2010: 313–35) uses tools of symbolic logic to put this consistency framework into a "formalized ethical theory." It also gives a thirty-five-step formal proof of GR in logical symbols.

[17] Of course, these groups don't share my *GR formulation* (which gives a philosophically defensible formulation of their GR insights).

- *Technical*: As rational beings decide how to act on important matters (and as they form related desires or moral beliefs), they ought as far as practically possible to be vividly aware of the relevant facts and to avoid falsehoods.
- *Simplified*: Be vividly aware of the facts and avoid falsehoods.

I'll divide this into *"Be informed"* (get the facts straight – believe truths but not falsehoods) and *"Be imaginative"* (exercise imagination – have a vivid awareness of the facts).

This section sketches an *ideal* of practical rationality which, even though it goes beyond our abilities, points us in the direction that we need to go, at least for important decisions.

Be informed. As far as practically possible, we need to know the situation, alternative moral views, and ourselves.

(1) We need to know the situation: circumstances, alternatives, consequences, and so on. To the extent that we're misinformed or ignorant, our thinking is flawed. An exception to this is that it may be desirable to eliminate information that will bias or cause cognitive overload.

(2) We need to know alternative moral views and arguments for or against them. Our thinking is less rational if we're ignorant of opposing views.

(3) We need self-knowledge. We can to some degree neutralize our biases through understanding how they originated. For example, some people are hostile toward a group because they were taught this when they were young. Their attitudes might change if they understood the source of their hostility and broadened their experience. If so, then their attitudes are less rational – since they exist because of ignorance.

Of course, we can never know *all* the facts; and we often have no time to research a problem and must act quickly. But we can act out of greater or lesser knowledge. Other things being equal, a more informed judgment is a more rational one.

Be imaginative. As far as practically possible, we need a vivid and accurate awareness of what it would be like to be in the place of those affected by our actions. This differs from just knowing facts. So in dealing with poor people, besides knowing facts about them, we also need to visualize and appreciate what these facts mean to their lives. Movies, literature, and personal experience can help us to visualize another's life.

We also need to appreciate the future consequences of our actions on ourselves. Knowing that drugs have harmful effects differs from being able to imagine these effects in a vivid and accurate way. A factual study about drug addiction might give us the facts, while a story or movie about drug addicts might bring these facts to life for us.

Kita (Know-Imagine-Test-Act) is an acronym to help us remember four main elements for using GR wisely:

K.   *Know*: "How would my action affect others?"
I.   *Imagine*: "What would it be like to have this done to me in the same situation?"
T.   *Test* for consistency: "Am I now <u>willing that if</u> I were in the same situation then this be done to me?"
A.   *Act* toward others only as you're willing to be treated in the same situation.

Here's an example. There once was a coal-mine owner named Rich, who grew rich by paying his workers almost nothing and grabbing all the profits for himself. Now Rich one day went through a moral conversion and decided to try to run his mine wisely according to GR. What would he do? Following Kita, he'd do four things.

(K) Rich would gain *knowledge*. He'd ask, "How are my company policies affecting others – workers, neighbors, customers, and so on?" To know this, Rich needs to spend time talking with workers and others.

(I) Rich would apply *imagination*. He'd ask, "What would it be like to be in the place of those affected by these policies?" He'd imagine himself as a worker (laboring under bad conditions for a poor salary), or a neighbor (with black smoke coming into his house). Or he'd imagine his children being brought up under the same conditions as the workers' children. Again, doing this may take considerable time and effort.

(T) Rich would *test* his consistency by asking: "Am I now <u>willing that if</u> I were in the same situation (as my workers, neighbors, or customers) then I be treated that same way?" If the answer is no, then his actions clash with his desires about how he'd be treated in a similar situation – and he must change something. Changing company policies requires *creativity*; he has to imagine and explore different possibilities. GR doesn't tell Rich which alternative policies to consider. Instead, it gives a way to *test* proposed policies. Any acceptable policy must be one he can approve regardless of where he imagines himself in the situation: as owner, worker, neighbor, or customer. The final solution will likely be a compromise that's minimally acceptable (but not ideal) from everyone's perspective.

(A) Rich would *act* on GR: "Treat others only as you consent to being treated in the same situation." Yes, it's a simple formula. But applying it wisely requires *knowledge* and *imagination* – which may be difficult. We'll never do knowing and imagining perfectly; but this doesn't excuse us trying to doing it as well as we reasonably can.

4.6 GR and Love-Your-Neighbor

How does GR ("Treat others as you want to be treated") relate to "Love your neighbor as yourself"? There are several plausible views about this. The *equivalence* view claims that both mean the same thing.[18] One might argue for this as follows:

> "Love your neighbor as yourself" = "Take your self-love as the model of how to treat others."
> "Take your self-love as the model of how to treat others" = "Treat others only as you're willing to be treated in the same situation."
> ∴ "Love your neighbor as yourself" = "Treat others only as you're willing to be treated in the same situation."

GR then spells what "Love your neighbor as yourself" means.

The *complementarity* view sees GR and the love norm as different but as working together. GR is about *procedure*; when combined with knowledge and imagination, it gives a way to help us decide how to act. "Love your neighbor" is about *motivation*; it means "Act in order to do good and not harm to your neighbor – and this for the sake of your neighbor." Ideally, we'd use both together:

Love-your-neighbor is the highest *motivation* for following GR. Some follow GR from lower motives, like social conformity or self-interest. It's better to follow GR because we love (care about) others for their own sake.

GR gives a *procedure* to operationalize love-your-neighbor. GR (with Kita) translates love into action. So if we love our children in the GR way, we'll try to *know* them (including their needs and desires), *imagine* ourselves in their place, and treat them only in ways we're willing to be treated ourselves by a parent in the same situation.

So then love gives a *motivation* (caring about others for their own sake) and GR gives a *procedure* to translate this into action.

---

[18] See Aquinas (1274: I–II, q. 99, a. 1) and Telushkin (2006–9).

The equivalence and complementarity views both seem sensible philo-sophically and consistent with the Bible; I know of no objective way to decide between them. But perhaps even better is a *combination view* that combines procedure with motivation. Here to love your neighbor is to do two things: to treat your neighbor as you want to be treated (GR proce-dure) and to do this because you care about your neighbor for his or her own sake (love motivation). I like this view the best, because it has the whole package: action and motivation. So when I speak of human love or of God's love for us, I'll usually have in mind this combined view.[19]

4.7 God and Natural Law

Like Aquinas's treatise on natural law (1274), our chapter so far mentions *reason* much more than *God*. Believers and atheists might agree with what we've said about moral realism, practical reason, consistency, the golden rule, knowledge, imagination, and so on. But atheists and believers would differ when relating these ideas to their respective worldviews.

Many atheists believe that the universe started with a big bang nearly 14 billion years ago; the universe moved from a hot dense state, through the formation of planets, the beginnings of life, and the evolution of humanity. Behind the universe, there's no great mind or underlying moral purposes; instead, the whole process came from amoral forces, like ran-dom variation and survival of the fittest. These amoral forces gave human-ity a primitive moral sense – since small, genetically similar clans who used the golden rule to promote cooperation had better survival chances. Thus an amoral universe, itself completely indifferent to moral concerns, brought forth humans with a sense of right and wrong.[20]

Atheists and believers can share the part of this account that's based on science, like the big bang and evolution, including the evolutionary origin of our sense of right and wrong. To this scientific core, atheists add *negative metaphysical beliefs* (that behind the universe there's no great mind or underlying moral purposes) while believers add *positive metaphysical beliefs* (that a loving and moral God created this evolv-ing universe for moral purposes). So both atheists and believers add

---

[19] Each part can justify the other part. GR leads to love-motivation, since we want others to follow GR toward us because they care about us. And love-motivation leads us to follow GR, as a way to operationalize this motivation.

[20] See Gensler (2013: 125–35), which also mentions other discussions about how evolution gave us a GR moral sense.

additional metaphysical beliefs that go beyond the scientific story.[21] I'll later argue (§§8.6–8.7) that the theistic additions are more plausible and reasonable than the atheistic additions.

Believers who accept natural law think that atheists can have a genuine morality, but that belief in God provides a worldview much more congenial to and supportive of a deeper morality.

The theistic NL worldview sees our origin and purpose in moral and religious terms. We have our source in a God who is perfectly wise, loving, and good. Calling God "good" doesn't mean that he fulfills his own desires; instead, it means that his life accords with inherent truths about goodness – for example, that love is good in itself and hatred is bad in itself. God created us in such a way that our minds can know the good and our wills can freely choose it. God intends that our moral struggles purify us and lead us toward our ultimate goal, which is eternal happiness with him. In contrast, atheists think that humans sprang up in a universe ultimately indifferent to moral concerns.

Theistic NL sees basic moral truths as true in themselves. Believers and atheists both can use their God-given reason to know these truths. But divine revelation about morality can be useful, since our minds are often clouded. While reason can tell us that stealing is wrong, we also can learn this through the Bible, the church, or prayer. Atheists as well as believers can know moral truths; but believers have additional ways to arrive at the same truths.

Believers also have additional motives for doing the right thing. An important motive is gratitude to God and love for his creatures. Doing the right thing is thus linked to our personal relationship toward God; doing evil offends God and hurts our relationship to the God who has been so good to us.

Believers and nonbelievers will mostly come to the same moral beliefs, for example, that stealing is wrong. But there may be differences. Believers will recognize a duty to worship God while nonbelievers won't. And there may be differences about issues like mercy killing, based on differences in beliefs about the origin and destiny of our lives.

Theistic NL relates God to morality, but more through *God's creation* than through *God's desires* (as in DCT). Our duties depend on how God

---

[21] Some unsophisticated atheists (Plantinga 2006 gives examples) present their negative metaphysical beliefs as if they're part of the scientific story.

created us – as beings of a certain sort, with a certain nature. God created us with a threefold nature, as rational, biological, and spiritual:

1. *Rational*: creatures with genuine but limited rational abilities (to form beliefs, draw conclusions, avoid falsehoods, recognize inconsistencies, imagine situations, have goals and desires, deliberate about actions, choose freely between alternatives, and so on)
2. *Biological*: members of the *Homo sapiens* species
3. *Spiritual*: called to eternal life with God

Our duties "flow from" our God-given nature – not in the sense that these duties are strictly deducible from a nonevaluative description of who we are – but rather in the sense that practical reason shows that a being of this nature has these duties. The "nature of X" in this context is the set of facts about X that practical reason needs to have to determine how X ought to act. The next chapter shows how this works.

I propose that our moral duties are of three kinds. (1) Some, like ones about consistency and GR, are duties that we have as *rational* beings; this is the present chapter. (2) Other duties, like ones about stealing and marital fidelity, are duties that we have as rational beings who are also *biological* beings of the *Homo sapiens* species (for whom possessions and sexuality, for example, are important); this is Chapter 5. (3) Still other duties, like ones about trusting in and worshipping God, are duties that we have as rational *Homo sapiens* creatures who are also *spiritual* beings called to eternal life with God; this is Chapter 6.

In terms of having genuine duties at all, our rational nature has a certain priority – since we couldn't have genuine duties without the ability to form beliefs, deliberate about actions, choose freely between alternatives, and so on.

This present chapter talked about our *rationality duties*. As we make important decisions, we ought, as far as is practically possible for beings of our sort, to be vividly aware of the relevant facts, avoid error, and be consistent (especially about GR and ends-means). All rational beings have these duties; we'd have these same duties if we were rational Martians or angels. We have these duties because God made us to be rational beings, in his "image and likeness."

But our likeness to divinity is incomplete. Our rational abilities are weak. Even our most reflective decisions are contaminated with much ignorance and falsehood. We daily struggle with ends-means consistency (in acting on our goal to moderate our eating) and golden-rule consistency (in how to treat someone who aggravates us). We know we can do better. Humans are feeble but called upon to be like gods.

God could have made our rationality stronger or weaker. Imagine these two possibilities:

- *Maxi-humans* are like us, but with *much more* wisdom and self-control. They have greater knowledge and empathy, believe fewer falsehoods, and have fewer inconsistencies. They more easily act on their goals and follow GR.
- *Mini-humans* are like us, but with *much less* wisdom and self-control. They're very ignorant, have little empathy, believe many falsehoods, and are filled with inconsistencies. It's difficult for them to even occasionally act on their goals or follow GR.

God made us somewhere between maxi- and mini-humans. He preferred to create moderately weak humans who struggle to know and do right rather than strong maxi-humans who needn't struggle.

5

Natural Law and Biology

On our natural law moral realism, our duties flow from our nature, using practical reason. Humans have a triple nature – rational, biological, and spiritual:

1. *Rational*: As rational beings, we're subject to norms of practical reason. In making decisions, we need to be vividly aware of the facts, avoid falsehoods, and be consistent (golden rule [GR], ends-means, reflective equilibrium, etc.).
2. *Biological*: As rational members of the *Homo sapiens* species, we have additional duties.
3. *Spiritual*: As rational creatures called to eternal life with God, we have additional duties.

This chapter focuses on our biological nature. We'll look for biological facts that lead, using practical reason, to general norms about how we, as human beings, ought to live.

On both divine command theory (DCT) and natural law (NL), our biological nature is from God and our duties are based on God's desires and purposes. But the views explain this differently:

- DCT: God creates humans in a certain way, because he has certain purposes for us. He then desires that we act in certain ways. *Our duties come directly from God's desires.*
- NL: God creates humans in a certain way, because he has certain purposes for us. *Our duties come from our God-given nature using practical reason.*

On NL, our duties come from how God *created* us.

5.1 Biological Human Nature

I was camping at remote Boucher Creek in the Grand Canyon, pondering a big question: "What is *human nature*? What is it to belong to the *Homo sapiens* species?" As I was thinking deeply, a squirrel came to my campsite, sniffing for food. I imagined the squirrel answering my question.

Squirrel Boucher began, "Judging from backpackers who camp here, humans are strange creatures. They're so unsuited to nature that they can survive only by taking a great number of things with them, which they load on their backs. It's comical to see these pitiful creatures stumble along on the trail, using only two legs, carrying so much weight! They bring food, water, clothes, shoes, shelter, tools, and so forth. They need such things to survive. Squirrels don't need any of this. If you drop a naked squirrel into a random wilderness without gear, it'll likely survive well. If you drop a naked human into a random wilderness without gear, it'll likely die. And yet some scientists think humans are the most evolved of all animals! This is foolish rubbish; squirrels and most other animals are more suited to their environment than humans.

"Consider food. Backpackers carry a pound and a half (seven hundred grams) of food per day, which is produced through a wide human network. Much of it needs cooking, so they need a pot, stove, and fuel; this weighs so much that it's difficult to bring food for more than a few days. On the other hand, we squirrels eat local nuts and berries that we find. If these aren't available, we eat vegetation, insects, eggs, small birds, or oatmeal cookies stolen from hikers (located using our acute smell); and we can easily climb trees to get more food. We seldom go hungry and never need to carry food. Hey, who is more evolved here?

"Humans in the Grand Canyon carry water, lots of it, or else they may die in the desert heat. And they purify stream water, using contraptions bought from other humans. We squirrels just drink from streams or munch on vegetation.

"Humans wear clothing and shoes, to protect them from hot or cold weather, rain, or rocky ground. My fur serves well for any weather conditions, and my feet don't need shoes.

"Backpackers carry tents, sleeping bags, and sleeping pads. I just sleep on the ground, or I make a little nest from leaves and twigs. Again, which of us is more adapted to the environment?

"Hikers bring other things, like backpacks, hiking poles, permits, maps, books, flashlights, electronic gismos, and so on. It must take thousands of humans to outfit a single hiker; all this is needed just to spend a single night at Boucher Creek! We squirrels need none of this.

"Human babies are born weak and helpless, and remain so for a long time; I'm surprised that any survive to adulthood. Older children also need careful attention and education; I've seen this with camping families – which usually are close-knit and include a mother, father, and children. In contrast, squirrels are promiscuous, live alone, and don't form families; squirrel mothers care for babies for several weeks, but squirrel fathers aren't involved. Squirrel reproduction is easier.

"On the positive side, humans are unusually intelligent and cooperative. Humans are very social, working together in many ways – setting up tents, cooking food, and getting water. They chat almost continually, to coordinate efforts, warn of danger, and enjoy each other's company. We squirrels don't need any of this; we do fine without setting up tents, speaking, or socializing. While human intelligence and cooperation are impressive, humans need these for survival just because they're so poorly suited, in almost every other way, for life on this planet. So humans are weak and poorly adapted, but they partly make up for this by their intelligence and ability to work together."

Squirrel Boucher did well (for a squirrel) in describing human nature and how we differ from most other animals. He nicely explains how possessions, speech, and family have an importance for us that's rooted in our biology. But he doesn't appreciate the higher aspects of human life: ethics, religion, art, music, books, friendship, and so forth. And he says little about our dark side: how we can wallow in ignorance and hurt each other. Of course, no description of human nature is complete; there's always more to say. But Boucher's comments can nicely introduce how our biology affects how we ought to live.

5.2 Practical Reason Again

Chapter 4 discussed practical reason's RAT norm (about facts, imagination, and consistency), which applies to us as rational beings. Now we'll explore how it applies to us as biological beings of a *Homo sapiens* nature. I'll make five points.

(1) RAT is the first duty of a rational being; but it's also a biological imperative for Homo sapiens. To survive and prosper, we need intelligence and cooperation – facts, imagination, consistency, ends-means, and GR. We can formulate this as a hypothetical imperative, where the goal

is one that we much desire: "If we want to survive and prosper (either as individuals or as a species), then we ought to develop practical reason."

Squirrel Boucher nicely summed up how weak and poorly adapted to nature humans are: "If you drop a naked squirrel into a random wilderness without gear, it'll likely survive well. If you drop a naked human into a random wilderness without gear, it'll likely die." He ends: "So humans are weak and poorly adapted, but they partly make up for this by their intelligence and ability to work together." Practical reason is about being intelligent (based on knowledge, imagination, and ends-means reasoning) and cooperative (GR helps people to work together instead of fighting). We humans need practical reason to offset our biological weaknesses.[1]

Squirrels, with easy access to life's necessities, needn't be so intelligent or cooperative. To survive and prosper, squirrels must move quickly, climb well, and hide from enemies; but they needn't have deep skills for thinking or cooperation.

To appreciate GR's social value in promoting survival and a tolerable life, consider Thomas Hobbes's (1651) imagined "state of nature" – where humans are totally egoistic, amoral, and without social rules. Life in this state would be miserable for everyone, since people would steal, lie, kill, or rape whenever this suited them, and cooperation would be impossible. Hobbes (1651: 108) argued that a tolerable life requires that we follow social rules that are summed up in "Do not that to another, which thou wouldest not have done to thy selfe"; with this, we can work together. A GR society better serves our needs.[2]

Humans would have died out long ago without GR cooperation; global warming may still destroy us (Pope Francis 2015), unless we learn to treat future generations as we want to be treated. We can't survive and prosper as isolated individuals, but only as social beings who work together; so

---

[1] Darwin (1871: 156–57) noted how our physical weakness helped to promote intelligence and sociability. "An animal possessing great size, strength, and ferocity, and which, like the gorilla, could defend itself from all enemies, would probably, though not necessarily, have failed to become social; and this would most effectually have checked the acquirement by man of his higher mental qualities, such as sympathy and the love of his fellow-creatures. Hence it might have been an immense advantage to man to have sprung from some comparatively weak creature. The slight corporeal strength of man, his little speed, his want of natural weapons, etc., are more than counterbalanced, firstly by his intellectual powers, through which he has, whilst still remaining in a barbarous state, formed for himself weapons, tools, etc., and secondly by his social qualities which lead him to give aid to his fellow-men."

[2] Hobbes's state of nature, however, is biologically impossible, since humans would have died off without social cooperation; human babies, for example, require intense love from others, especially mothers, to survive.

evolution built a tendency toward GR altruism into us (Gensler 2013: 131–35).

Believers may sense a divine purpose behind our biology. Because we're so ill adapted to our environment, we needed to develop wisdom and love to survive and prosper.[3] God designed our biology to push us to develop our personhood and thus our likeness to God (who is supremely wise and loving). We can see this, for example, in how God made humans so that infants and children need great care and nurturing.

(2) Many psychologists use the idea of *cognitive dissonance*. We tend to be distressed when we find we're inconsistent. So when students discover that that their first sentence is inconsistent with their last, or that their goal to be a doctor clashes with their actions, they feel distress; and they scramble to rearrange their beliefs, desires, and actions to fit together. Cognitive dissonance also applies to GR; we're distressed when our action toward another clashes with our desire about how we'd be treated in a similar situation. Festinger (1957: 3) sees avoiding inconsistency as a basic motivation (see also Aronson 1969):

> Dissonance...is a motivating factor in its own right.... Cognitive disso-
> nance...leads to activity oriented toward dissonance reduction just as hunger
> leads to activity oriented toward hunger reduction. It is a very different moti-
> vation from what psychologists are used to dealing with but, as we shall see,
> nonetheless powerful.

Since inconsistency brings confusion and blocks intelligence, consistency promotes survival. Cognitive dissonance likely comes from our evolution and is reinforced by socialization. This would help explain how RAT's consistency component is somehow "written on the human heart" (to use the traditional phrasing) or "hard-wired into our genes and brains" (to use the equally colorful evolutionary phrasing).

One might similarly argue that we have an inherent motivation to gain facts relevant to our choices, display these vividly in our minds, and avoid errors – and that evolution put this into us for survival advantage. I'm normally motivated to change my views or actions if I believe any of these:

- "I'm inconsistent."
- "I'd decide differently if I had more information."
- "My decision is based on factual errors."

---

[3] I read this long ago in Pierre Teilhard de Chardin, a French Jesuit who influenced a whole generation of Christians to take evolution more seriously.

- "I'd decide differently if I visualized my action's effects."
- "My action hurts others."

Such RAT motivations are likely biologically based.

(3) Human nature is rational, but with a limited and weak rationality. We're limited in our ability to know the facts, be vividly aware of them, avoid falsehoods, and be consistent. Rationality norms have to be qualified to apply to us (*"as far as practically possible,"* and so on, §4.2.2). And we often struggle with *being* rational (§4.7) – for example, acting on our goal to moderate our eating (ends-means) or treating politely someone who aggravates us (GR). It's an important part of human nature that such things are so difficult for us.

Humans have a messy mix of warring motives – including positive ones, like rationality and altruism, and negative ones, like selfishness, greed, lust, pride, and revenge. So yes, GR is built into us; but so are strong contrary motives. Humans are weak and often must struggle hard to do the right thing.

(4) Subsidiary norms of practical reason apply to us in light of our human nature (§4.2.6). As social beings who learn better together, we need to *dialogue with others*; this is important to develop knowledge and imagination, and expose inconsistencies. As emotional beings, we need to develop *feelings that support practical reason* – like a passion to get the facts straight, a hatred of falsehoods (including false stereotypes), and deep feelings of concern for people. So *Homo sapiens*'s social and emotional nature deeply influences its rational-animal existence.

(5) While GR can be based on abstract reasoning (§4.4), its *importance* in human life is based on an empirical fact about human nature: we tend to be self-centered. This is perhaps our greatest problem. Judging from GR's omnipresence, this self-centeredness problem exists across different cultures and eras. GR deals with the problem, not by directly telling us what to do, but by hitting the ball back to us: "How am I willing that I be treated in the same circumstances?"

We can imagine rational beings for whom GR is less important. Suppose that Martians, while otherwise like us, follow GR naturally and without struggle. But they forget to get the facts about how their actions affect others – or maybe they ignore their own interests and treat themselves as doormats. We'd then expect Martians not to emphasize GR (since they live it so completely) as much as some other norm, perhaps "Be factually informed" or "Have regard for yourself too." So GR's central importance in human life is contingent on a fact about human nature: we tend to be self-centered.

5.3 Four Commandments

When we apply practical reason to generate norms for beings of our biological nature, four key norms stand out: "You shall not steal, lie, kill, or commit adultery." These are seen across the globe as centrally important. They're part of the Judeo-Christian Ten Commandments (§1.3) and of the Parliament of the World's Religions' "Declaration for a Global Ethic" (Küng 1993); the latter, like my view, bases these on GR, which it calls "the irrevocable, unconditional norm for all areas of life." NL sees such norms as accessible to everyone's reason, regardless of religious beliefs.[4]

These four commandments apply, not to all rational beings, but to those with a human biology. We can imagine angels who lack possessions (and so can't steal from each other), who know all truths (and so can't lie to each other), who can't die (and so can't kill each other), and who aren't sexual (and so can't commit adultery). And squirrels lack possessions, can't speak, and don't form pair-bonds. Since our commandments are important for *human* life, their justification needs to bring in *Homo sapiens* biology. It also needs GR; we're so built that we aren't willing that others steal, lie, kill, or commit adultery against us in typical cases; so consistency pushes us toward general rules against such actions.

To justify these commandments more systematically, we'd first try to understand *Homo sapiens*'s need for possessions, speech, life, and family. Then we'd consider possible rules of action. To test a rule, we'd see how it would affect various parties in typical situations, imagine ourselves in their place, and ask, "Am I now willing that if I were in the same situation then this be done to me?" We'd look for rules that we're willing to have followed in typical situations, regardless of where we imagine ourselves or others in the situation – and this after getting factual knowledge and exercising our imagination, as well as we practically can (§§4.2–5). The commandments are summaries of what practical reason prescribes and should be interpreted and applied using practical reason.

These four norms are rough guides to key areas. They apply clearly to *typical* cases but not to all conceivable cases. Individual societies need

---

[4] These four norms, with GR, also get high marks from Kinnier 2000, which summarizes scientific research about ethical universals (see §5.5.5), and from the *Atheism for Dummies* guy (McGowan 2013).

practical reason to create laws and customs that more concretely specify and apply a norm like "You shall not steal" to their cultural situation. To bind us morally, human rules must be for the common good, made by one who has care over the community, and promulgated; human rules that violate NL are unjust and so not genuine laws at all.

These four commandments protect centrally important areas of human life – possessions, speech, life, and family – that we need to survive and prosper. Individuals, for individual gain, often attack these – by stealing, lying, killing, and adultery; the commandments forbid this. These four norms cover not all duties but only some key ones; they omit duties about reparation, gratitude, obedience, human rights, just social structures, helping those in need, developing talents, and so forth.

Now we'll go through these four commandments individually.

(1) *You shall not steal.* Squirrel Boucher, while not needing possessions himself, was amazed at all the things that human backpackers carry: food, water, clothes, shoes, shelter, tools, and so forth. Humans need such things to survive and prosper; they suffer if they lose their possessions.

What about humans stealing from other humans – taking another backpacker's food or shoes or tent, for example? Should we consider this permissible? Consider the effect on the person stolen from – and what it would be like to go hungry, climb out of the canyon without shoes, or spend the night without a tent – because someone stole your things. And having your things stolen brings psychological trauma. Am I now willing that if I were in the place of the person whose things are stolen, then my things be stolen? Surely not! So I can't consistently hold that such stealing is permissible. Insofar as I consistently support a norm about stealing, which I'll want to do to protect my own interests, I'll hold that stealing is wrong.

My example is about stealing from a backpacker; examples about other cases would go in a roughly similar way. If I look for a rule about possessions that I'm willing to have followed, regardless of where I imagine myself or others in the situation (after getting factual knowledge and exercising my imagination), I'll accept a rule *against* stealing.

I won't end up with an *exceptionless* duty not to steal under any conceivable circumstances. Following practical reason, I'd allow a starving person to steal a loaf of bread, when needed, from someone who has much bread but refuses to share; I'm willing that I be stolen from under such circumstances. A commandment like "You shall not steal" is intended as a rough guide that holds "other things being equal," in normal cases. For controversial cases, we have to apply practical reason (including facts, imagination, and GR) directly to the case – and individuals may sometimes come to different conclusions.

A thief typically wants to gain possessions without working for them. Both sides will likely suffer. The stolen-from person suffers loss of possessions, psychological trauma, time spent trying to get possessions back, and time spent guarding possessions. And the thief will lose self-worth, live in fear of getting caught, and perhaps suffer social disapproval and go to jail. Stealing is a disease that harms everyone in the vicinity.

A commandment like "You shall not steal" can also lead to further reflection and refinements. What rules about stealing, and punishments for stealing, should the state have? If people steal because they're too poor, is this a sign that we need to educate the poor to get better jobs and reduce the gap between rich and poor? Is taking advantage of immigrants, paying them very little for work, *stealing* from them? Is taxing the rich more to help the poor (maybe to provide job training) wrongful *stealing* – or is it having everyone contribute his or her fair share for the social good? If people steal because they excessively love possessions, what attitude should we have toward possessions? Should we try to get as many as we can ("Those with the most toys when they die win") – or should we use possessions to serve higher values (like sharing and helping others)?

While a rough guideline like "You shall not steal" is beyond dispute, specific cases often get muddy. Aquinas spoke of this muddiness problem (1274: I–II, q. 94, a. 4):

Although there is necessity in the general principles, the more we descend to matters of detail, the more frequently we encounter defects.... The natural law, as to general principles, is the same for all.... But as to certain matters of detail, which are conclusions, as it were, of those general principles, it is the same for all in the majority of cases... and yet in some few cases it may fail.

It's a weakness of my approach, and of every other approach, that it doesn't clear up all the controversial cases. We can clear up many cases by getting the facts straight and applying imagination and GR. But often getting the facts straight is beyond our abilities, and our practical reason may still leave issues muddy. But that's life; we can only do as well as we can. My approach's strength lies in its focus on practical reason – how it works and its *usefulness and limitations* for limited rational beings like us. My approach leads to a *responsible moral autonomy*, where the rough guidelines are clear but have to be applied using our practical reason to life's difficult cases.

So a commandment like "You shall not steal" is a blunt instrument, a rough formulation that on reflection needs refinements and qualifications. Such blunt instruments have great value for the moral life. We likely do ninety-nine percent of our moral thinking using them, and they serve us well. The moral life would be intolerable if we had to reason in detail about every mundane action. And such commandments give a strong presumption against certain actions; so we must work hard if we want to justify a particular act of stealing.

(2) *You shall not lie.* Speech is important to human life. Squirrel Boucher, who doesn't use language, was impressed at how humans "chat almost continually, to coordinate efforts, warn of danger, and enjoy each other's company." Speech also promotes practical reason (by helping to spread knowledge, correct errors, spur imagination, and point out inconsistencies) and thus the good of society.

Lying typically promotes the liar's good at the expense of such social goods. Lying typically manipulates people, using them to get what we want without showing them consideration. Since we don't want to be lied to in normal situations, practical reason pushes us toward a general rule against lying.

"You shall not lie" is a rough rule that holds "other things being equal," in normal circumstances; it isn't intended to apply to all possible cases. It's surely right to lie about where your friend is to a madman who wants to find and kill your friend. And it may be right to tell a trivial "white lie" (like "Yes, dear wife, I really love your new shoes") rather than cause great distress. For controversial issues about lying, we have to apply practical reason (including facts, imagination, and GR) to the particular case[5] – and individuals may come to different conclusions.

"You shall not lie" is a rough guideline that can lead to further reflection and refinements. What rules about lying should the state have? (I'm thinking of cases like perjury, false advertising, and false reporting of income.) Is it permissible to tell a big lie to promote the social good? Does this strategy usually backfire; and even if it didn't, would lying still be wrong? Need we always tell the whole truth, or can we keep quiet about some things? Is keeping quiet sometimes equivalent to lying? Is it right to use misleading language, which leads people to believe falsehoods, even though we don't directly assert a falsehood?

---

[5] Carson (2010) shows in detail how to apply a GR-based practical reason to a wide range of difficult cases that involve lying.

(3) *You shall not kill.* Our lives are fragile, and we have strong survival instincts. Humans spend much energy trying to survive; this involves shelter, healthy food, doctor visits, police and military, locking doors, and avoiding dangers. We try to protect our lives, and we don't want to be killed. So practical reason (including GR) will push us to forbid killing.

People kill for various misguided reasons, including greed, revenge, ideology, and wars of aggression. There are also controversial areas, like capital punishment, self-defense, mercy killing, suicide, and abortion. And should the norm against killing also be taken to forbid physical and mental harm? As with other commandments, the rough "You shall not kill" is widely accepted but with many disputes. For controversial cases we may need to apply practical reason to the case – and people may come to different conclusions.[6]

When should we take a norm as very strict, or even as exceptionless? I suggest: "Take a norm more strictly if doing so would tend to prevent great evils or foolish choices." Here "great evils" cover things like the killing of an innocent person, the bringing about of a drug addiction, or the ruining of a happy marriage. When such things are at stake, and when following a looser rule is apt to lead to bad choices, it makes sense to follow a strict or even exceptionless rule. For example, "Just say no" would better serve someone tempted to take drugs than would a complex rule that can be easily twisted. Many problems come from taking moral rules so loosely that we can talk ourselves into doing almost anything. (See Gensler 2011a: 128–30.)

(4) *You shall not commit adultery.* Humans differ much from squirrels in sexuality and family life. Squirrels are promiscuous, live alone, and don't form families; squirrel mothers care for babies for a short time, but fathers aren't involved. While some humans prefer this model, human reproductive biology is far different. Our babies are born weak and helpless; they remain so for a long time, requiring extraordinary care. Older children also need careful attention, of an intensity and duration unparalleled in the animal kingdom. Children need so much care that it's difficult for a mother to do it well by herself; children brought up without a father are much more likely to suffer psychological problems, poverty, poor schoolwork, drug abuse, and criminal behavior. So humans

---

[6] I've argued (Gensler 1986; 2011a: 168–75) that GR consistency favors the belief that abortion is wrong in at least most cases. While the details are complicated, I argue that most people won't be consistent if they hold that abortion is normally permissible – since they won't consent to the idea of themselves having been aborted in normal circumstances. But this argument, even if it succeeds at what it tries to do, still leaves some details fuzzy.

evolved strong family life; the deepest emotional bonds for most humans are familial: husband-wife, parent-child, sibling-sibling, and so on. For most humans, family contributes more to happiness and life satisfaction than anything else; this is how we're built, unlike squirrels. Evolution worked hard that humans would find family life attractive – not just sex but also family bonds, since both are needed for the next generation to survive and prosper.

Marital infidelity is the biggest enemy of family life – breaking families, destroying deep relationships, hurting those we love, and especially harming children. We don't want to be on the receiving end of these actions; so practical reason (including GR) will lead us to forbid marital infidelity.

But again, "You shall not commit adultery" raises controversial issues. Is adultery permissible if there are no children and if husband and wife both agree to it? Is it permissible if the marriage is already dead? What about arranged marriages, divorce, contraception, premarital sex, polygamy, and gay marriage? What role should the state have to regulate marriage? Is there one answer to these questions that all societies should follow, or can different societies rightly follow different models, with the goal of promoting family life best in their cultural situation? For controversial cases we have to apply practical reason (including facts, imagination, and GR) to the particular case, keeping in mind the interests of children and the importance to human happiness of deep family relationships.

The deterioration of families is a big problem and very harmful for children and society; we've moved too much toward a model of sexuality and family life suited more for squirrels, for whom family bonds and raising children aren't important (see Gensler 2011a: 158–59). Since many so easily talk themselves into adultery ("No one will find out and it will cause no harm"), and since the harm done by adultery can be so great, I urge that we uphold very strictly the duty not to commit adultery.

We shouldn't be too optimistic that these four norms will ever be *universally* followed. We humans are weak, fallen, and subject to strong counterinclinations (like selfishness, greed, and lust). The moral life is a struggle.

5.4 Intrinsic Goods

I've appealed to what's needed for humans to prosper (lead a good life) or what brings harm. So now I have to discuss *intrinsic good*, which is about the *value of a life* (§3.3.1).

Aquinas (1274: I–II, q. 94, a. 2) saw "good" in terms of natural human inclinations (desires):

All those things to which man has a natural inclination are naturally apprehended by reason as being good, and consequently as objects of pursuit, and their contraries as evil, and objects of avoidance.

But we have natural inclinations to bad things too – like selfishness, laziness, and revenge – so we can't simply equate "good" with "what we have a natural inclination for." Aquinas (1274: I–II, q. 94, a. 4) himself raises this objection and responds:

Objection: Now different men are naturally inclined to different things; some to the desire of pleasures, others to the desire of honors, and other men to other things.

Response: As, in man, reason rules and commands the other powers, so all the natural inclinations belonging to the other powers must needs be directed according to reason. Wherefore it is universally right for all men, that all their inclinations should be directed according to reason.

This suggests that we base *good* on *what's rational to desire* – what we'd desire if we satisfied practical reason as far as practically possible (§4.2). So we'd first try to be vividly aware of the relevant facts, avoid falsehoods, and be consistent; and then we'd see what we desire for its own sake.

If we apply practical reason to decide what things are good in themselves, what do we get? Here are some possibilities:

1. *Hedonism*: All pleasure is *intrinsically good* (good in itself, abstracting from consequences), all pain is *intrinsically bad*, and nothing else is intrinsically good or bad. Painful things, like going to the dentist, can be *extrinsically good* (good because of consequences) if they bring future pleasure or prevent future pain. Value depends entirely on the *amount* of pleasure or pain; a life is better if it brings about a greater balance of pleasure over pain.

2. A *pluralistic view* (Gensler 2011a: 117–18): Many things are good in themselves, such as virtue, knowledge, pleasure, life, and freedom. These need qualifications: it isn't good in itself to have pleasure over another's misfortune or to have knowledge of trivial facts.

3. John Finnis (2011: 57–99): The basic values are life, knowledge, play, aesthetic experience, friendship, practical reasonableness, and religion. Since these can't be measured on a common scale and totaled, the utilitarian duty to *maximize* total value is senseless.

Instead, we're free to choose which basic goods to emphasize. Choosing directly against a basic good, however, is always wrong; this leads to exceptionless norms (for example, against murder, which violates the basic good of life).

4. NL thinkers give other lists of basic goods (see Murphy 2011). Aquinas mentions rationality, knowledge, life, procreation, and society. Others add integrity, justice, pleasure, avoiding pain, health, family, work, inner peace, excellent activity, or happiness.

While all of these seem to be goods, it's difficult to say which are "intrinsic" (or "basic"). It mostly doesn't matter. For example, *family* is a great good in human life – and so adultery, which attacks it, is a great evil; and this holds regardless of whether family is a basic value (to be valued for its own sake) or a derived value (to be valued because it promotes virtue, knowledge, life, friendship, happiness, and so on).

To respond to the problem of evil (§§8.1–3), believers need to reject hedonism and to value highly a virtue that comes after a difficult and free struggle.

5.5 Further Issues

Now we'll consider some further questions and challenges about my NL view.

(Q1) I'm skeptical about independent moral facts. It seems that every fact must assert either a state of matter or a state of mind. But no independent moral fact would do either. So there can't be independent moral facts. Besides, such moral facts would commit us to an old fashioned Platonism, with Platonic forms and such.

Let's express the first argument more carefully:

> Every fact asserts either a state of matter or a state of mind.
> No independent moral facts assert either a state of matter or a state of mind.
> ∴ There are no independent moral facts.

Here premise 1 is self-refuting (since it can't itself assert either a state of matter or a state of mind). And the argument assumes that a certain abstract inference form is valid (All F is B or C, Nothing that is F and M is B or C ∴ No F is M); but *the fact that this form is valid* doesn't assert a state of mind or a state of matter. So the argument is self-refuting again. In addition, deductive reasoning seems to presuppose that *we ought to avoid inconsistencies* (or else why not accept the premises but reject the conclusion of a valid argument?), which I've argued is best seen as an independent moral fact (§3.9).

Since I'm unclear about Platonic forms, I've explained moral realism without using such ideas (§3.9), basing my definition instead on that of the antirealist Carson (2012: 467):

Strong moral realism holds that there are moral facts about the value of actions (including oughtness, permissibility, and goodness) that hold independently of actual or hypothetical facts about will (desires, commands, approvals, and so on), including divine and human will.

I agree with Carson that moral realism and anti-realism are both plausible, with no knock-down arguments on either side; so I've defended theistic ethics on both views. But I favor moral realism, which I think makes better sense of central moral claims. And I suspect that any clear argument against moral realism (such as the one given above) is objectionable on other grounds. Arguments against moral realism tend to be based on overly restrictive preconceptions about what all facts must be like, often using natural science as a model for all reality; such preconceptions, when expressed clearly, can be seen to be self-refuting and inadequate for other parts of our knowledge.

(Q2) Are there other arguments against moral facts?

Yes, I'll consider six more (most are self-refuting).

1. Logical positivists argued this way (Ayer 1946: 102–20):

   Any genuine truth claim has to be either analytic (true by language conventions, like "All bachelors are single") or testable by sense experience (like "There's snow outside").
   No statement asserting an independent moral fact is either analytic or testable by sense experience.
   ∴ No statement asserting an independent moral fact is a genuine truth claim.

Logical positivism (premise 1) has now been almost universally abandoned, since (1) it's self-refuting (it's neither analytic nor empirically testable, and so on its own terms isn't a genuine truth claim), (2) the difference between what is or isn't empirically testable proved impossible to draw in a clear way, and (3) many things that positivism declares not to be genuine truth claims are very sensible (as in the next example).

2. Some argued for emotivism (the view that moral judgments are emotional exclamations, like "Boo!" and "Hurrah!") over moral realism in this way:

> Any view is better if it's simpler and explains more.
> Emotivism is simpler and explains more than a moral realism that accepts
>   independent moral facts.
> ∴ Emotivism is better than a moral realism that accepts independent moral
>   facts.

Emotivism, they claimed, can easily explain why "good" (being emotional) can't be defined using (neutral) descriptive terms, why we can't prove (emotional) moral conclusions from just descriptive facts, why we can't intellectually resolve basic moral differences (which are emotional), why we differ so much in our moral beliefs (because our emotions differ), and why we're motivated by moral beliefs (because they're emotional). Emotivism appeals to something simple – positive and negative feelings – and avoids ideas that are difficult to understand or defend, like independent moral facts. So emotivism, being simpler and explaining more, is the better theory.

However, emotivism doesn't explain morality adequately; by denying moral knowledge and truth, it *explains away* morality and violates common sense. Also, emotivism would take premise 1 ("Any view is *better...*") to say "Hurrah more for views that are simpler and explain more!" So premise 1 wouldn't be a truth claim; this destroys the argument. Emotivism also destroys the rationality of science, since norms of scientific method (like "Any view is *better* if it's simpler and explains more" and "We *ought* normally to believe our sense experience") become exclamations, and no more objectively true than "A view is *better* if it accords with my horoscope."

Emotivism has other problems. Complex moral sentences translate poorly into exclamations; so "Either A is good or B is bad" would have to translate into the senseless "Either hurrah for A! or boo for B!" And unemotional moral judgments can't plausibly translate into exclamations.

3. David Hume (1739: 457) attacked moral realism on the basis that moral ideas motivate us (influencing our actions and affections) while reason and facts of themselves are impotent:

> All moral ideas motivate us.
> Nothing that expresses a fact motivates us.
> ∴ No moral ideas express a fact.

Premise 2 is false. Given a desire to win, we can be motivated by the fact that scoring a quick goal is needed to win. Premise 2 needs to say, "Nothing that expresses a fact motivates us *independently of our desires.*" Then we have to change premise 1:

> All moral ideas motivate us *independently of our desires.*
> Nothing that expresses a fact motivates us *independently of our desires.*
> ∴ No moral ideas express a fact.

Premise 1 is then doubtful. Moral ideas may motivate us just because of our desires (to be consistent, avoid cognitive dissonance, treat others rightly, obey God, gain eternal life, or whatever; §6.5.1). We could imagine someone lacking such desires who has no motivation to follow moral ideas.

4. Gilbert Harman (1977: 6–23) noted that we use "observe" in both science and ethics. So scientist Sara, seeing a vapor trail in a cloud chamber, says, "I *observe* that a photon went by"; and moral philosopher Meg, seeing hoodlums burn a cat in gasoline, says, "I *observe* that this act is wrong." Sara and Meg take their experiences to confirm a belief about an external fact. Sara is right in doing this, but Meg is wrong. To explain Sara's observation, we have to consider the fact that a photon *did* go by. To explain Meg's observation, however, we have to consider only her psychological makeup; assumptions about moral facts (that the act is wrong) are irrelevant to why Meg made her observation. The *best explanation* of our experiences involves positing scientific facts but not moral facts. So it's reasonable to believe in scientific facts but not moral facts.

Here's one way to express the argument:

> The best explanation of our experiences involves positing scientific but not evaluative facts.
> If the best explanation of our experiences involves positing scientific but not evaluative facts, then it's reasonable to believe in scientific but not evaluative facts.
> ∴ It's reasonable to believe in scientific but not evaluative facts.

But premise 1 ("The *best...*"), if true, expresses an evaluative fact. So the argument inconsistently uses evaluative facts to reject evaluative facts. Here's another formulation:

> All genuine facts explain our experiences.
> No moral facts explain our experiences.
> ∴ No genuine facts are moral facts.

Again, premise 1 is self-refuting, since the truth or falsity of "All genuine facts explain our experiences" won't explain our experiences. So, on its own terms, premise 1 can't express a genuine fact. And there are other factual statements whose truth or falsity doesn't explain our experiences – like "Any view is *better* if it's simpler and explains more" or "Some planets beyond our communications range contain thinking beings."

Philosophy needs to look for the best explanation of our broad, commonsense views about the world (which posits facts about material objects, scientific theories, other minds, mathematical truths, *and moral truths*), and not just the best explanation of our sense experiences. To think otherwise is to confuse philosophy with empirical science.

5. J. L. Mackie (1977: 36–42) gave two arguments against objective values. His *argument from relativity* considers variations in moral codes between societies, historical periods, and social classes. We can explain these variations better by taking them to reflect different life styles rather than different perceptions of objective values. If we directly perceived moral truths, as we perceive colors or perhaps mathematical axioms, then there'd be a greater uniformity in moral beliefs than what we find when we study anthropology.

Mackie here attacks a *perception* model of moral knowledge, whereby we just look at and see moral facts. I reject this too and instead see moral knowledge as based on practical reason.[7] We differ in our moral views mostly because we imperfectly apply the elements of practical reason: getting the facts, exercising imagination, and being consistent. Our scientific and moral beliefs follow a similar pattern: we first absorb such beliefs from our society, and then we may use our reason to criticize these beliefs and move to better ones over time.

6. Mackie's *argument from queerness* claims that objective values, if they existed, would be entities or qualities of *a very weird sort*, utterly different from anything else in the universe. And our knowledge of such values would require a special faculty of moral perception or intuition, utterly different from ordinary ways of knowing. So moral realism consists of weird, strange, and peculiar ideas – and so is better avoided.[8]

Weirdness is subjective. Consider *matter* ("This is a chair"), *mind* ("I feel pain"), and *math* ("$2 + 2 = 4$"). If we take any of these as the norm

---

[7] It's difficult to see how evolution could give us the ability to directly perceive moral truths; it's easier to see how it gave us the abilities needed for practical reason (§§5.2, 5.5.11–12).

[8] Jordan (2013a) and Mavrodes (1986) use this to defend DCT over NL.

to which all knowledge must conform, then the others seem weird. As we read Descartes and take immediate experience as the norm, matter and math seem weird and need justification. In materialist moods, everything must be reduced to matter (including mind and math) – while in mathematical moods, matter and mind are suspect because they don't rest on necessary truths. Mackie says most thinkers accept objective values; these seem weird *to him* (*but not to them*) because he takes matter and math as the norm to which all knowledge must conform. But why do this? And don't even matter and math bring weird ideas, like charmed quarks and transfinite numbers? Everything leads to weirdness if we push it far enough.

Mackie presupposes a premise like "There are no facts beyond kinds X, Y, and Z" (where these give areas that he finds acceptable). What kind of fact does this unstated premise assert? It doesn't assert a fact about the physical world. Nor does it likely express a fact of kind X, Y, or Z. But then this unstated premise expresses a weird kind of fact, not of the allowed kinds, and so becomes self-refuting. So Mackie's argument, when expressed clearly, becomes self-refuting.

My basic NL norms are norms of *practical reason* – about being vividly aware of the relevant facts, avoiding error, and being consistent. *Theoretical reason* (for areas like science and math) requires similar norms – about getting the facts, avoiding error, and being consistent; rejecting these would bring intellectual suicide. On what basis could we reject the norms of practical reason as being "weird" without also rejecting the very similar norms of theoretical reason?

Mackie (1977: 23, 31) and others see moral objectivity as part of our philosophical tradition, our ordinary thinking, and our moral language; so they think it has a strong presumption in its favor. But then, if the contrary arguments are weak (as I've argued they are), we should accept moral objectivity.

(Q3) Are there similar arguments against belief in God?

Yes, there are several, for example:

- The existence of God cannot be a fact about the physical world – and these are the only facts that there are.
- Claims about God aren't either analytic or testable by sense experience – and so are meaningless.
- We can explain the world more simply by using science without God; and so accepting science and rejecting God is the more reasonable explanation (but see §§8.5–6).

- God, if he existed, would be an entity of a very queer sort, utterly different from anything else in the universe, and hence is to be rejected.

Such arguments can be criticized in much the same way as the analogous arguments against moral facts.

Nonbelievers who come to believe in objective moral facts sometime convert to theism later (examples include Augustine, C. S. Lewis, and Patrick Glynn). Since the same ideas that attack moral facts may also attack belief in God, making room for objective moral facts may also make room for God.

(Q4) How many natural moral laws are there?

I distinguish three groups. My *rationality group* has only the RAT norm. This could divide into three or four norms (be informed [seek truth and avoid falsehood], imaginative, and consistent). Consistency could divide into consistency in beliefs, consistency in will, conscientiousness, impartiality, GR, and so forth; my logic textbook (Gensler 2010: 290–335) gives a formal system that can generate an endless set of consistency norms.

My *biological group* has four key norms, against stealing, lying, killing, and adultery. These could divide into more-specific norms. Further norms could be added, based on GR, about reparation, gratitude, obedience, human rights, just social structures, helping the needy, developing talents, and so forth.

My *spiritual group* in the next chapter has only one law: "Love God with your entire being." This could divide further.

(Q5) Are some natural moral laws nearly universally accepted across the globe?

Yes, GR and norms against stealing, lying, killing, and adultery are nearly universal. Here's some evidence:

- At the 1993 Parliament of the World's Religions, representatives of the world's religions overwhelmingly approved a document, which they saw as expressing their own values, that supports GR and these four commandments (see Küng 1993; Gensler 2013: 57–59).
- Kinnier (2000) summarizes a large amount of scientific research about ethical universals. While GR was seen as the clearest and most impressive universal value, norms against stealing, lying, and killing were also included.[9]

---

[9] The norm against adultery is mentioned but didn't make his short list. But it's nearly universal if we admit cultural differences (e.g., about polygamy).

Gensler 2013 (34–66, 76–107) has more on the common moral core (especially GR) in the religions and cultures of the world.

The four norms that are nearly universal are *rough guidelines*. Different cultures may implement them in ways that are different but still make sense. These guidelines become less clear when applied to controversial cases; NL recognizes this (§5.3) and suggests that we apply practical reason as best we can to such cases (even though we may not reach agreement).

Kinnier lists other values that are nearly universal. Two of these, to seek truth and to act in harmony with conscience, are part of my rationality norm. Further items (like self-discipline, helping and forgiving others, and avoiding gluttony and greed) could be added to my biological duties. My spirituality norm about loving God is widespread but less universal, since some don't accept God; Kinnier and the Parliament of the World's Religions have vaguer forms of this that speak of being committed to an "ultimate reality" or a "higher transcendental purpose."

Natural law and modern social science claim that some values are *"nearly* universal" or known by *"virtually* everyone." We need the italicized qualifications for three reasons.

1. Small children, the comatose, and mentally defectives may not have the capacity to grasp these moral norms.

2. Some unusual groups may lack these moral norms. Turnbull (1972) described the Ik people as coping with starvation by becoming cruel and amoral; while his descriptions are disputed, human society clearly can turn to the dark side, as in Nazi Germany. So the moral values that are so common across humanity aren't totally universal.

3. Some may lack the moral concepts. Even "2 + 2 = 4" isn't totally universal, since some primitive tribes who count "One, two, three, many" supposedly lack the concept *four*. But still, "2 + 2 = 4" is *nearly universal* in humanity. Most generalizations about humans are about what is *nearly universal*.

Most of us use a range of moral concepts, including flavors of *right-wrong-ought*, *good-bad-better*, *praiseworthy-blameworthy*, *virtuous-vicious*, and *rights*. Simpler societies may have fewer moral concepts. There could perhaps be societies that have no genuine moral concepts but instead express norms more crudely, as perhaps "X is punished" or "Boo on X!" It's difficult to imagine a human society with no norms, not even such crude ones; but such societies may be possible.

Extreme cases shouldn't make us reject the important truth that there's a *nearly universal agreement*, across ages and cultures, on some central values. But still, if we speak of morality as "written on our hearts" (Romans 2:13–15), we shouldn't think of it as written in big, bold letters.

(Q6) Is your NL view foundationalist or coherentist?

The rational level is foundationalist; it's based on the self-evident RAT norm, from which GR and other consistency norms can be deduced. The biological level is coherentist; we look for norms we can hold consistently in light of knowledge and imagination. The spiritual level is partly based on faith.

(Q7) Does your NL view support norms that hold always (in all cases)?

Yes, there have to be such norms, but they can be hard to formulate. A friend proposed "*Never* burn a child in gasoline just for fun." I objected that it could be permissible to burn a child in a low-burning-temperature gasoline (if there were such a thing) if this were harmless and the child enjoyed it. We can fix the norm by adding a few words: "Never *severely hurt* a child by burning it in gasoline just for fun." Another plausible exceptionless example is "*Never* kill anyone just for the person's political beliefs" (see Gensler 2011a: 128–30).

(Q8) Immanuel Kant (1785: 76) objected that basic moral norms must hold for all possible rational beings, and so a NL that builds basic moral norms on the peculiarities of human nature must be mistaken. How do you respond?

Humans have a threefold nature: *rational, biological,* and *spiritual.* Having a rational nature, we're subject to practical-reason duties that apply to all rational beings; Kant was a leader and inspiration in this area. But we also have other duties, such as not to steal, which applies practical reason to our biological nature (unlike squirrels, we need possessions to survive and prosper); Kant underestimated the need for empirical knowledge about our nature to help ground such duties.

(Q9) Some use NL to argue that contraception and homosexual activity are *unnatural* and hence wrong. Since *the natural function of sex is reproduction,* genital sexual relations are morally proper only when occurring between husband and wife in a sexual intercourse open to procreating children. Do you accept this reasoning?

No. I've never in this book argued that something is wrong because it's unnatural. While I've argued for strong norms about sex (§5.3.4), my reasoning is different from this. I have four problems with this natural-function argument.

1. I'm unclear what "The *natural function* of sex is reproduction" means, especially since it's supposed to have such strong moral implications. Is this claim about the *built-in goal* of the biological act? Why think that biological acts literally have built-in goals, especially ones that are always wrong to act against? Or is the claim about *what God intends the act to be used for* (which is more DCT than NL)?

2. If we think biological actions literally have built-in goals, then why take sex to have just one function (reproduction) instead of two (reproduction + pair-bonding)? Unprotected human intercourse brings pregnancy only about 3 percent of the time, in part because it usually happens at nonovulating times; females of most other species are sexual active only when their bodies are in a state to make pregnancy possible. Why the difference? Some think we evolved this way to promote pair-bonding (important for raising children) through regular sex; this idea favors the two-function view.

3. Even if we grant that sex has *one natural function* (or maybe two), we still need another premise to conclude that using sex for anything else while blocking this one function (or maybe blocking one of the two functions) must be wrong. In general, it needn't be wrong to use organs for something other than their primary biological purpose (like using our feet to kick a football). So why must it be wrong to use sex for something other than its primary biological purpose?

4. Basic NL norms are written on the human heart and known to virtually everyone (§4.1) – unlike the controversial "It's always wrong to act against a natural function."

Although the *natural-function* argument is often attributed to Aquinas, the prominent NL thinker John Finnis (1997) rejects this and claims that it's better, and truer to Aquinas, to base the same conservative sexual norms on how sex contributes to a good human life (and especially to the good of marriage).

(Q10) David Hume (1735: 475) objected to NL that, since the word "natural" can have so many senses, it's unphilosophical to base morality on what's natural. When we say that selfishness is a *natural inclination*, we mean that it's common and not socially learned. Or we might speak of *natural ingredients* (not artificial), *natural explanations* (not miraculous), or *natural knowledge* (not supernaturally revealed). In none of these senses is the natural always better than its opposite.

Hume's point is less a refutation of NL than a reminder that we need to make clear what we mean by "natural" in a given context. So I explain "natural" in the phrase "natural law" (§4.1) in terms of evolutionary instincts and capacities that are "written on the human heart" (as opposed to being based on divine revelation or social convention).

(Q11) So how can evolution explain how these NL norms are "written on the human heart"?

Charles Darwin (1871) talked about how social animals (like dogs, wolves, ants, and bees) have instincts that lead them to work together, help each other, and sympathize with another's distress or danger. With social animals, evolution encourages instincts and behaviors that benefit group survival.

Humans are social animals, living in families or groups. Like other such animals, we evolved social instincts. We enjoy helping others and are distressed by another's misery. We show concern for others, especially offspring and members of our group. We value the approval of others, internalize group values, and follow the leader. Opposing our social instincts are antisocial instincts, like lust, greed, vengeance, and divisiveness.

According to Darwin, primitive humans had arbitrary taboos, little discipline, and little concern for those outside one's clan or tribe. As humans developed, rationality and religion gradually purified our social feelings and moral instincts. We struggled toward a higher morality, supported by reason and directed to everyone's good, including the weak and animals. Our noblest attribute became a love for all living creatures. GR sums up this higher morality: "Treat others as you want to be treated."

I'd go with Darwin here, using evolution to explain how moral principles are written on the human heart (instincts); I'd add that God uses evolution to write moral principles on our hearts. The evolutionary story has got more complicated since Darwin – especially with the rise of genetics and sociobiology (with ideas like *kin altruism, reciprocal altruism,* and how GR is *hard-wired into our genes and brains*). And other sciences can contribute here, including neuroscience, psychology, and sociology (for a longer discussion, see Gensler 2009; 2013: 66, 111–14, 127–29, 131–38).

So evolution instilled in us a tendency to think and act in accord with the basic norms of practical reason (RAT), including GR. From these, plus descriptive knowledge, we arrive at norms against stealing, lying, killing, adultery, and so on.[10]

(Q12) Do you really think that evolution can explain how humans came to know moral truths? Some believers argue that the evolution + atheism combo would give us thinking mechanisms that reliably produce, not true beliefs, but beliefs with survival value.

Yes. As I see it, the key issue is whether evolution would have instilled in us the basic norm of practical reason (RAT):

As you make important decisions, do what you reasonably can to be vividly aware of the relevant facts, avoid falsehoods, and be consistent (GR, ends-means, etc.).

Humans have a strong motivation to be consistent; psychologists study this in terms of *cognitive dissonance* (§5.2). We also have a strong motivation to gain the facts relevant to our choices, display these vividly in our minds, and avoid errors. Practical reason has great survival value, and so evolution would have instilled into us a tendency to follow it.

While this seems plausible, two theistic philosophers have raised technical problems that relate to this explanation.

1. Alvin Plantinga (2011: 307–50) argues that evolution and atheism fit together poorly. On the evolution + atheism combo, it's unlikely that our thinking mechanisms would reliably lead to beliefs that are *true* instead of ones that merely *promote survival*. And so we'd have little reason to accept any of our beliefs as true, including beliefs about evolution. So this combo leads to intellectual suicide. Believers don't have this problem, since they can see God as guiding evolution[11] so that it gives us thinking mechanisms that reliably lead to true beliefs.

---

[10] Since I use RAT + regular empirical knowledge to justify further moral claims, I don't need to explain how humans evolved a capacity to *perceive* or *intuit* further moral truths. This would indeed be difficult to explain.

[11] God could guide evolution by controlling externally random mutations. Since quantum physics permits a range of random outcomes, none uniquely determined by previous conditions, such divine activity needn't violate laws of physics. Plantinga (2006: 206) says, "Clearly a mutation could be both random in this [external] sense and also intended and indeed caused by God. So the fact, if it is a fact, that human beings have come to be by way of natural selection operating on random genetic mutation is not at all incompatible with their having been designed by God and created in his image. Perhaps, for example, God orchestrates the whole process, causing the right mutations to show up at the right times, intending a certain result."

I'm not sure whether Plantinga is correct here; the issue is complicated. If he *is* correct, then atheists should quickly switch to being believers. And then they can accept both evolution and my claim of a few paragraphs ago – that evolution (but then guided by God) instilled practical reason's basic norm into us.

2. Angus Ritchie (2012: 40–66) argues that theism explains our moral knowledge better than atheism. I'll express his argument in my own way. Compare *groupism* ("Have concern just for the good of your group") with *universalism* ("Have concern for everyone's good"). Let's assume that groupism is objectively wrong while universalism is objectively right. Now if atheism were true, then evolution would have instilled in us groupism, which has greater survival value in the battle between tribes. But believers and atheists alike know that groupism is wrong. And so only if a loving God somehow guided evolution would we have had universalism instilled into us.

I have doubts about Ritchie's argument. Darwin thought *biological evolution* instilled groupism into us but *cultural evolution* (including the rise of reason and religion) later moved us to universalism, as expressed in GR.[12] I'd explain it this way (Gensler 2013: 138). Biological evolution put into us both groupism and a call to consistency that contains the seeds of GR. After many years of cultural evolution, GR developed enough in our minds to challenge groupism and move us to a GR universalism (see §§4.4–5 and Gensler 2013: 136–51). Three further cultural factors kept moving us away from groupism:

- Wise leaders come to see that groupism, by promoting a war between groups, hurts *every* group, and that universalism better promotes the good of *all* groups.
- As groups in complex societies mix (through processes like intermarriage), group identity becomes less well defined.
- Religions increasingly teach moral universalism.

---

[12] Darwin (1871, Chapter 4) wrote, "To do good in return for evil, to love your enemy, is a height of morality to which it may be doubted whether the social instincts [from biological evolution] would, by themselves, have ever led us. It is necessary that these instincts, together with sympathy, should have been highly cultivated and extended by the aid of reason, instruction, and the love or fear of God [by cultural evolution], before any such golden rule would ever be thought of and obeyed." Later he talks about how our intellectual powers [over time] "naturally lead to the golden rule, 'As ye would that men should do to you, do ye to them likewise'; and this lies at the foundation of morality."

While groupism is still strong throughout the world, and is built into our genes and instincts, evolution can, if we include cultural evolution, explain the rise of universalism.

Despite what I say, Ritchie's basic thesis may be right. Ritchie compares his reasoning to the fine-tuning argument (§8.6). Perhaps the circuitous biological + cultural story that led to GR universalism is more likely in a universe created by a loving God who intended to create creatures with such a morality.

The evolution + atheism combo has another problem. Consider sophisticated achievements of human intelligence: science, engineering, math, religion, philosophy, ethics, logic, art, and so on. Consider that our brains developed under crude conditions, fighting for survival in the jungle. Isn't our intelligence an overkill, enormously more than what's needed for jungle survival? What's the likelihood, in an atheistic world, that a thinking capacity evolving in primitive ape-like creatures would eventually reach such sublime heights? Isn't this much more likely if we assume that a loving God engineered evolution to produce creatures in his image and likeness, creatures intended to rise ever higher in personhood over time?

(Q13) Let's assume that there are objective, independent moral truths (moral realism). Why think that rationality tracks these truths? Why suppose that, by becoming more rational (informed, imaginative, and consistent), we're more likely to arrive at moral truths?

This is perhaps an unavoidable presupposition: we just have to assume that becoming more rational in an area makes us more likely to arrive at what's true in that area.

Maybe theism helps here. God so designed our minds that we can, by becoming more rational (more wise and loving), come better to know the truth about how we ought to live. And if we assume that God (having supreme rationality) is morality's ultimate judge (§6.4), then growing more like God (in rationality) may move us closer to moral truths.

(Q14) If there are intelligent, rational beings on other planets, would they likely believe in GR?

Yes. If such beings exist, which I think probable, they'd likely believe in GR, since (1) they likely evolved as we did, with their survival requiring a GR-like cooperation; (2) GR, as a central moral truth, would likely be accessible to them; and (3) God would likely have planted GR in their minds and hearts.

(Q15) Are there purposes in nature?

Purposes in the primary sense are always purposes of conscious individuals (like God, humans, and animals). In an extended sense, mere objects can have purposes that derive from primary-sense purposes; so if we say that a paper cutter has the purpose of cutting paper, we mean that individuals who make or use paper cutters have this purpose.

In human beings, *is the purpose of the eye to see*, in a sense beyond that this is what humans typically use the eye for? Atheists and theists should answer this question differently:

- *Atheists*: "Evolution resulted in a diversity of beings, and those with eyes often survived better because they were able to see; so evolution led to many beings having eyes. But there's no *purpose in nature* here, except metaphorically; we wrongly anthropomorphize nature if we say that it literally gave us eyes *in order that* we might see."
- *Theists*: "Yes, evolution resulted in a diversity of beings, and those with eyes often survived better because they were able to see; so evolution led to many beings having eyes. But a purposeful God used evolution to bring it about that we have eyes to see. And so, in a deeper sense, we can say that the (divine) *purpose* of our eyes is that we may see."

So theists, in speaking of purposes in nature, could be speaking of *divine purposes* in nature.

6

Natural Law and Spirituality

On our theistic natural law, our duties depend on our God-given nature –
as rational, biological, and spiritual beings:

1. *Rational*: Be vividly aware of the relevant facts, avoid falsehoods,
   and be consistent (GR, ends-means, etc.).
2. *Biological*: Avoid stealing, lying, killing, adultery, etc.
3. *Spiritual*: Love God with your entire being.

We'll now investigate the basic spirituality duty and see what this adds
to morality.

6.1 A Spirituality Norm

I'll express the *supreme spirituality principle* (SPR) in two ways. The first
is a *qualified ought-form*:

SPR: If there's a God (in the sense of a supremely wise and loving Creator),
then rational creatures who are called to eternal life with God ought, as far as
practically possible, to love God with their entire being.

The duty to love God is contingent on there being a Creator who is
supremely wise and loving, and calls us to eternal life with him; this duty
wouldn't apply, for example, if the world had no Creator or else had
one like the hateful Ares (§3.1). SPR's second formulation is a *simplified
imperative form*:

SPR: Love God with your entire being.

The first form is more technically precise; the second is easier to read. I'll move freely between the two forms (with the technical form's qualifications being implicit in the simpler form).[1]

Here I take "wise" to mean "satisfies the norms of practical reason" (§4.2.7) and "loving" to mean "satisfies GR and cares for others for their own sake" (§4.6). God's wisdom and love include these, but likely go much further.

Atheists could accept SPR as purely hypothetical: *if* there's such a God (which they reject), *then* we ought to love him with our entire being. Here I'll assume that there *is* such a God. I won't worry about the status of this assumption – whether it can be based on human reason or must instead be based on revelation. If it requires revelation, then the duty to love God isn't part of *natural law* (as we've defined it) but rather is part of *supernatural law*, and then this discussion is theological rather than philosophical.

The duty *to love God with our entire being* is comprehensive, covering all aspects of our lives.

(1) Loving God with our entire being requires *obeying God* – doing what God wants us to do. Our other duties, given that God wants us to follow them, are also obedience duties. Thus obeying God fulfills all our duties.

Religion personalizes morality. When we steal, lie, or break the golden rule, we do something that's wrong on nonreligious grounds; but we also disobey God and *sin* against the One who loves us and created us. (*Sin* is an intentional violation of God's will; atheists can accept wrongdoing but not sin.) So morality connects to our personal relationship with God.

Why should we obey God? Here are four reasons:

- God, having perfect knowledge, knows all our duties, and, being consistent in will, wants us to follow them all. So if we do God's will, then we follow all our duties.
- We humans, being limited in wisdom and love, ought to take the highest wisdom and love as the measure of moral action. But the highest wisdom and love is God. So we ought to take God as the measure of moral action, and obey God.

---

[1] SPR may *partly* apply if there's a wise and loving Creator who *doesn't* call us to eternal life with him. I'll here work with the stronger assumption.

- The lower should depend on the higher. Just as our lower, animal, bodily nature should be ruled by our higher, rational nature – so also we, as limited beings, should be ruled by the supremely highest being, who is God.
- By obeying God, we promote our ultimate happiness, which is to be found in eternal life with God.

I argued previously (§2.7.3) that obeying God needn't violate the *responsible moral autonomy* that we rightfully want for ourselves – especially if God's will for us is mostly very general. Indeed, our NL commandments give only a general outline of our duties. God wants us to work out the details, using knowledge, imagination, and the golden rule. So we have much moral thinking to do for ourselves.

(2) Loving God with our entire being requires *loving our neighbor and following the golden rule*. Since God's commandments include "Love your neighbor" and "Treat others as you want to be treated," this is a corollary from the first point:

> Loving God requires obeying God.
> Obeying God requires loving our neighbor and following GR.
> ∴ Loving God requires loving our neighbor and following GR.

Loving our neighbor and following GR is the most important part of loving and obeying God. An important corollary is, "You shall not pervert God's goodness by making God and religion into forces that promote hatred and divisiveness."

Also, when we love a person deeply, we come to care about those whom that person loves. So when we love God deeply, we come to care those whom God loves (everyone).

GR has a significant but different presence in the three dimensions of our nature:

1. *Rational*: GR is a consistency duty and plays an important role in rational thinking about moral issues. We can be motivated to follow GR by seeing that it's right and rational and treats fellow rational beings with respect.
2. *Biological*: We humans, while weak and poorly adapted to nature, have great intelligence and capacity for social cooperation. GR, which evolution put into us, is essential if we're to survive and prosper. We can be motivated to follow GR by seeing that others are fellow human beings, flesh of our flesh.

3. *Spiritual*: GR is a divine imperative and part of God's plan for us to grow in personhood toward our eternal fulfillment with him. We can be motivated to follow GR by love of God and gratitude to him, and by seeing that we're all children of one God, made in his image and likeness.

Theistic morality is richly multidimensional.

(3) Loving God with our entire being requires *living the other two theological virtues* (the greatest being love):

- *Faith* is believing in God and what he has revealed.
- *Hope* is emotionally trusting in God and his promises.
- *Love* is striving to serve God and, as part of this service, to do good and not harm to his creatures.

These are traditionally seen as supplementing the *four natural virtues* from ancient Greek philosophy: *wisdom* (governing ourselves by reason, whereby we understand how we ought to live and we act on this); *courage* (facing danger and fear with proper confidence); *temperance* (controlling our desires and emotions); and *justice* (dealing fairly with others).

(4) Loving God requires following the first three of the Ten Commandments:

1. You shall not worship false gods.
2. You shall not take God's name in vain.
3. Keep holy the Sabbath.

Furthermore, we ought to pray – to lift up our minds and hearts to God, both as individuals and in community. We're called upon to worship the God of supreme wisdom and love, to live in his presence, to praise him in song, to ask his forgiveness and help, and to thank him for his many blessings.

Gratitude should motivate our response to God. The commandments in the Bible start with a prologue: "I am the Lord your God, who brought you out of Egypt, out of the land of slavery." Recalling the good that God has done for us, we're motivated by gratitude to respond in love, service, and obedience. Christians can also recall that the Son of God was sent to transform us through his suffering. And all theists can recall that our lives are a gift from God – and that even our suffering and struggles are meant to bring us closer to God.

(5) Finally, loving God with our entire being requires *that we praise and love God in other aspects of our lives*. If you're an artist, praise God

through your art. If you do science, praise God through your science. If you're a parent, praise God through your love for your family. If you hike the Grand Canyon, praise God through your hiking. If you struggle with faith, praise God through your struggles. Love, serve, and praise God with your entire being.

For believers, morality is part of loving God. That's the biggest difference that theism makes to morality.

One of the worst ways to connect ethics with religion is to see God as a judge who sets up arbitrary rules and then enjoys punishing us for breaking these rules. God is wise and loving, and open to forgive us when we stumble (as we will do).

The opposite error sees God as ultrapermissive, as if a loving God will let us get away with anything. But love isn't permissiveness – as a loving parent isn't a permissive parent. Those who are hateful and cruel toward others should feel great guilt; but again, God is open to forgive.

6.2 Why We Exist

C. S. Lewis (1952: 72) noted (my italics):

Morality, then, seems to be concerned with three things. Firstly, with fair play and harmony between individuals. Secondly, with what might be called tidying up or harmonizing the things inside each individual. Thirdly, with the *general purpose of human life as a whole*: what man was made for: what course the whole fleet ought to be on.

Christianity is bold about the purpose of human life. In Catholic grade school, I memorized these answers from the *Baltimore Catechism* (1941: 12):

1. *Who made us?* God made us.
2. *Who is God?* God is the Supreme Being, infinitely perfect, who made all things and keeps them in existence.
3. *Why did God make us?* God made us to show forth His goodness and to share with us his everlasting happiness in heaven.
4. *What must we do to gain the happiness of heaven?* To gain the happiness of heaven we must know, love, and serve God in this world.[2]

---

[2] Since this seems to keep atheists out of heaven, I'd add "as well as we can"; atheists can love and serve God (unknowingly) by loving God's creatures. The Catholic Vatican II (1962–65) in *Lumen Gentium* 16 says that God doesn't deny salvation by those who,

So what's the purpose of human life? It's *to show forth God's goodness and share everlasting life with God – which requires that we know, love, and serve God in this world.* Ignatius of Loyola (1524), with a different emphasis, said that man was created *to praise, reverence, and serve God our Lord, and by this means to save his soul.* I prefer to say that we were created *to love God above all things and our neighbor as ourselves, both in this life and in the next.*

6.3 A Genesis Story

In the beginning, before the universe was created, there existed only God. God was supremely powerful, wise, and loving; because he was supremely wise and loving, he was also supremely *good.* God existed in three persons – Father, Son, and Holy Spirit – in harmonious love and goodness.

God decided to share his love and goodness with others, by creating rational creatures in his image and likeness. But how would he create them? God rejected an easy solution: to create rational creatures fully formed and share his life with them. God decided instead that his rational creatures would struggle and grow through free choices, taking a long journey back to him (and to eternal life); he judged that a long, epic struggle toward the final fulfillment would ultimately be more meaningful.[3]

So nearly 14 billion years ago, God started creation with a tremendous explosion, a big bang. The event was carefully orchestrated. To eventually produce life, creation had to be very precise: the gravitational constant g, the "strong" nuclear force, the total mass of the universe, the expansion rate, and so on. With everything incredibly fine-tuned (§§8.5–6), God said, "Let there be light!" The explosion happened, it went well, and God said, "It is good!"

And so God started it all with the big bang. From an initial hot dense state, there was a sudden inflating explosion. Over a longer time span, stars formed, and then planets; there emerged a wide range of atoms, from helium to heavy metals, and compounds like water. On a small cooling planet called Earth, and likely on others as well, the material conditions needed for life came together. Then simple life-forms came into

through no fault of their own, don't explicitly know God but yet with his grace strive to live a good life.

[3] The early Christian thinker Irenaeus (c. 120–200), in explaining why we weren't created perfect, emphasizes the value of struggle: "The harder we strive, so much is it the more valuable; while so much the more valuable it is, so much the more should we esteem it. And indeed those things are not esteemed so highly which come spontaneously, as those which are reached by much anxious care." (Swindal 2005: 55) See also §8.1–3.

existence. Through random genetic mutations, these life-forms diversified; fitter ones survived and passed on their features. After billions of years, life-forms of high complexity and high inner awareness had emerged. And God said, "It is good!"

There still were no rational creatures made in God's image and likeness. So God, through evolution, brought forth primates who were weak and poorly adapted to their environment; to survive in a hostile environment, these creatures had to struggle to become smarter and more socially cooperative. And so humans gradually emerged; their primitive personhood had a tiny spark of divinity, a small likeness to God's infinite personhood. And God said, "It is good!"

Humans in time developed greater rational and moral capacities. They could form beliefs, imagine situations vividly, avoid falsehoods, and recognize inconsistencies. They could do ends-means reasoning. They could be concerned for others of their clan, treating them as they themselves wanted to be treated. They achieved moral notions like *good*, *bad*, and *ought*. They thus gained a primitive sense of right and wrong. They could choose between alternatives, using their gift of free will. So humans could choose to be more wise and loving, or, as they often did, to sink into ignorance and selfishness; they could choose to build up human society, or, as they often did, to tear it down. When humans struggled, against strong contrary urges and inclinations, to do right, this accorded with God's plan, for God treasured virtue reached after struggle.

Owing to our peculiar biology, we need many material things (like food, clothing, shelter, and tools); we need speech to promote our highly social living; we need respect for each other's lives and well-being; and we need intense family life (to form close bonds that further the upbringing of children). This all fits God's plan. But opposing forces push us toward stealing, lying, killing, and adultery – against God's plan. God intended that life be a struggle, but a highly meaningful struggle – since from this can emerge higher wisdom, love, and personhood.

God also gave us, perhaps through a "God gene," a hint of the eternal life to which we're called. By nature, we're religious, and we express this in diverse ways. God sent prophets to every nation, to teach us to choose between the way of darkness and the way of light. We're all on a journey, a search for self-understanding, a search for meaning and purpose, a search for happiness beyond what this life provides, a search for infinite wisdom and love, and ultimately a search for God.[4] And so God leads

---

[4] Alasdair MacIntyre (2009: 5–6) expressed it well: "Finite beings who possess the power of understanding, if they know that God exists, know that he is the most adequate object

us, as we fall and struggle to get back up, to grow more into his image and likeness, toward greater wisdom and love, and ultimately toward the eternal life to which he calls us.

6.4 A Hybrid View

Natural law, as developed so far, has a major problem. While this view emphasizes four key commandments, it leaves fuzzy their application to particular cases (§5.3). Aquinas (1274: I–II, q. 94, a. 4) gave this example: "We ought to return what we borrow when the owner wants it back" is a good general principle; but it can fail when we borrow a weapon that the owner wants back in order to cause evil. We can vary the case; maybe the evil goes from minor to major (from a water balloon hitting someone to an atomic weapon destroying a city) and is less or more probable (from 1 to 100 percent likely). Humans of fairly good moral rationality would in many cases disagree on what ought to be done. And there are many further controversial issues about stealing, lying, killing, and adultery (§5.3).

NL holds that *practical reason* is the measure of right action. But our practical-reason abilities are limited; for example, we seldom know about the long-range consequences of our alternatives. In such controversial cases, is there a correct answer (a truth of the matter) about right and wrong? What should NL say about this? We'll consider five options.

(Option 1) *In controversial moral cases, there are no correct or incorrect answers.* This gives up much of the objectivity of ethics; the only objectively true norms about human nature are general, vague ones like "You shall not steal." NL thinkers wouldn't find this attractive.

Option 1 also violates the common NL belief that there's a correspondence between our duties and God's commands:

Correspondence: If A is our duty, then God commands A.

Now imagine a controversial act B. Here one of these three alternatives will be true about what God commands:

1. God commands B.
2. God commands not-B.
3. God neither commands B nor commands not-B.

---

of their love, and that the deepest desire of every such being, whether they acknowledge it or not, is to be at one with God."

In these three cases, the correspondence principle given earlier would have implications about which actions are duties:

1. Suppose God commands B. Then, by the correspondence principle, not-B cannot be our duty (since then God would command not-B) – and so any human who thought not-B was our duty would be mistaken.
2. Suppose God commands not-B. Then, by the correspondence principle, B cannot be our duty (since then God would command B) – and so any human who thought B was our duty would be mistaken.
3. Suppose God neither commands B nor commands not-B. Then neither B nor not-B can be our duty (by similar reasoning), and so any human who thought that B was our duty or that not-B was our duty would be mistaken.

In any of the three cases (and one has to be true), there are some moral views that are *mistaken*; this is incompatible with option 1, which claims that there are no correct or incorrect answers on controversial moral issues.

(Option 2) *In controversial moral cases, there are correct answers; these are determined by what would be agreed on by all ideally rational humans (who know all relevant facts, are ideally imaginative, and are completely consistent).* This faces the Carson problem (§3.4): that it's physically impossible for humans to know all relevant facts about many issues (like which occupation to pick, where knowing all relevant facts would require an enormous brain); and even if we had such knowledge, we might still disagree on many issues.[5]

(Option 3) *In controversial moral cases, there are correct answers; these are determined by what most moderately rational humans would favor.* This raises the issue of how to define "moderately rational human," and it tends to make minority views automatically wrong. Also, given the correspondence principle, it would absurdly force a *supremely rational* God to go with what most *moderately rational* humans favor.

(Option 4) *In all controversial moral cases, there are correct answers; these are determined by moral facts that hold independently of actual or hypothetical facts about will (desires and so on), including the will of God and of humans.* This extreme moral realism seems doubtful, even to me. I find it easier to accept the RAT norm of practical reason

---

[5] This problem led Carson from full-information theories of rationality to a divine-preference view (§3.4). Here it leads me to a divine-preference NL.

as an objective, independent moral fact than to hold that every controversial moral issue is decided by its own objective, independent moral
fact.

(Option 5) *In controversial moral cases, there are correct answers;
these are determined by God (who is supremely rational, wise, and loving).* This seems to me to be the most plausible approach for theistic
natural law. If we accept option 5, as I think we should, we move to a
hybrid combination of NL and DCT. Let's call this "divine-preference
natural law" (DNL). Here the basic norms of practical reason (RAT) are
objective, independent truths that *roughly* determine right and wrong in
many cases; but controversial cases should be decided by a being of ideal
practical reason, if there is such a being.

An atheist version of my NL approach would reject option 5. Probably
option 1, which gives up much of the objectivity of ethics, is the most
plausible of the remaining options (but the extreme moral-realism option
4 is also possible).[6]

Accordingly, I add a second clause to RAT, to get RAT*:

RAT*: As rational beings decide how to act on important matters (and as they
form related desires or moral beliefs), they ought as far as practically possible:

A.   to be vividly aware of the relevant facts, avoid falsehoods, and be consis-
     tent, and
B.   for cases where A doesn't lead to a clear result because of limited rational-
     ity, to follow the will of a being who supremely satisfies A, if such a being
     exists.

Atheists could accept B as purely hypothetical: *if* there's such a God
(which they reject) *then* we ought to follow his judgment on controversial
cases. Theists, since they accept that God supremely satisfies A, could use
this simpler version of B:

B*. For cases where A doesn't lead to a clear result for creatures, to follow
     God's will.[7]

This hybrid NL-DCT view fits traditional NL ethics, which teaches
that vague NL norms can be further specified by suitable authorities
using practical reason; so a government might set up laws about what

---

[6] Boyd (1988) accepts a moral realism with limited bivalence (like option 1).
[7] A modified DCT version of this (mirroring §3.6) could say that "good action" means
  "action desired by the highest available wisdom and love" – where being wise and loving
  is seen as satisfying part (a) of RAT*, which includes GR. In practice, this would differ
  little from our DNL.

constitutes stealing. Now God, the supremely wise and loving Creator of the universe, surely has the moral authority to further specify vague NL norms. Aquinas defined "law" as "an ordinance of reason for the common good, made by him who has care over the community, and promulgated" (1274: I–II, q. 90, a. 4); this would apply to God deciding controversial moral issues (if we waive "promulgated").

This hybrid view also fits the traditional NL view that the measure of *right action* is *practical reason*. While human practical reason is limited and doesn't always speak with one voice, divine practical reason isn't so limited. Extending NL to DNL is very natural; and DNL may be to what some NL thinkers had in mind all along. And so DCT and NL come together.

On this hybrid DNL view, some of our duties are independent of God's will; these include RAT and GR. Our duty not to steal depends on God's will, but only because our human nature depends on God's creative will. Practical reason clearly determines that beings having our human nature generally ought not to steal; so our general duty not to steal is fixed by our nature (with no further need for God to decide that stealing is bad, once he decides on our nature). But God decides difficult cases about stealing when human reason can't agree on an answer.

On DCT our duties come directly from God's desires, while on NL our duties come from our God-given nature using practical reason (§5.0). My hybrid DNL says this:

DNL: God creates humans in a certain way, because he has certain purposes for us. Our duties come from our God-given nature using practical reason. We can know our basic duties through reason. But for difficult cases where our limited reason doesn't give a clear answer, we should see God, who has perfect reason, as making the final decision.

Why does morality need God, if right and wrong are decided by practical reason? Part of the answer is that morality needs God if it's to be well defined (so controversial moral questions have a right answer) and thus more thoroughly objective.

How would this hybrid DNL view answer the Euthyphro question? *Is a good action good because God desires it? Or does God desire it because it's good?* The answer depends on which good action we're talking about.

Rationality duties are based on RAT. As rational beings decide how to act on important matters, it's good that they be vividly aware of the relevant facts, avoid falsehoods, and be consistent. God desires these things because they're good; their goodness doesn't depend on their being desired by God. But, following Suárez (1612), such things can be good for another reason too, that they're done in obedience to God.

Human-nature duties are based on our God-given human nature using practical reason.[8] So the general goodness of respect for property, speech, life, and family depends on how God created us rather than on further divine desires. God desires these things for us because they're good for beings of our nature; they aren't good for beings of our nature because God desires them.

But God decides our duties when weak human reason cannot do this. Then an act A is good *because* God favors it. However, he favors A typically *because* his supreme reason favors it, and his supreme reason favors A *because* of facts about A. But then A's goodness comes, ultimately, not from God's will but from God's reason. And then our motive for doing A shouldn't be just that God desires it; we should also be motivated by the reasons why God desires it (e.g., how A benefits people).

Sometimes, however, an act's goodness may come more from God's will than from his reason. Suppose that practical reason determines that humans, from their need to nourish their spiritual nature, have a duty to worship God. God can arbitrarily decide that the main worship day be Sunday instead of some other day or no day at all; then the goodness of worshiping on Sunday depends on God's arbitrary decision. But such cases are perhaps the exception (see Evans 2013: 32–37).

Except for subtle conceptual points, my modified NL is rather close to Chapter 3's modified DCT, which identifies "good action" with "action desired by the highest available wisdom and love (God)." In practice, these views are more alike than different. And so many NL insights may apply to DCT, and many DCT insights may apply to NL.

6.5 Further NL Issues

Now we'll consider some further questions about my divine-preference natural law (DNL).

(Q1) What explains the *authority* of moral judgments?

---

[8] Our spirituality duties work like our biological human-nature duties. So our loving God is good because of our God-given spiritual nature.

On a *rational level*, an ought-judgment is authoritative because it's a truth that logically entails an imperative to do something. If I say "This man is bleeding," this may be true; but it entails no imperative to act in a certain way. If I say "I *ought* to call the doctor," again this may be true; but here this truth logically entails a "*Call the doctor*" imperative to act in a certain way. So if I accept the ought-judgment then, to be consistent, I have to accept the logically entailed imperative, and so act in order to do the thing in question. So if I accept the ought-judgment but don't act accordingly, then I'm inconsistent – and my life here loses coherence.

On a *biological level*, when I don't act on my moral beliefs (or when I act against them or violate GR), then typically I feel cognitive dissonance, I feel my incoherence as painful, I feel distress that I'm violating my beliefs, and I feel some motivation to change. Cognitive dissonance is a feeling and motivation that supports our rational and moral side; evolution put this into us, and society reinforces it for its own survival. So members of the *Homo sapiens* species tend normally to feel bad when they violate rationality or morality.

On a *spiritual level*, morality is authoritative for two further reasons. My wrongdoing pits me against God, who is (1) infinitely wise and loving (and thus the supreme moral authority) and (2) the ultimate source of my fulfilment and happiness. By the second point, morality is always in my self-interest.

(Q2) If our reason can distinguish right from wrong, then isn't revealed biblical ethics redundant and unnecessary?

In moral matters, faith and reason mostly say the same thing; for example, both command GR and forbid stealing, lying, killing, and adultery. Some might get moral norms from reason, others might get them from the Bible, and still others might get them from both sources. It's useful to have several places to get moral norms. Sometimes it takes much study to get moral norms from reason, and many people might not have the time or intellectual ability to do it; so they might do better to get moral norms from faith. Thus it's very useful that we can get moral norms both from reason *and* from faith.

Aquinas says this at the beginning of his *Summa Theologica* (1274: I, q. 1, a. 1), but about our knowledge of God: "Even as regards those truths about God which human reason could have discovered, it was necessary that man should be taught by a divine revelation; because the truth about God such as reason could discover would only be known by a few, and that after a long time, and with the admixture of many errors." In morality too, many of the truths that reason can discover would, without revelation, "only be known by a few, and that after a long time, and with the admixture of many errors." And revelation can tell us more about loving God, help us grow in this area, and give us a broader religious perspective for morality.

(Q3) How do moral theology and moral philosophy differ?

Moral philosophy appeals just to human reason while moral theology also appeals to revelation (including the Bible and Church teaching). Christian moral theology emphasizes

- *sin* (including forgiveness and reconciliation, temptation and moral struggle, grace and conversion, motivation, eternal life, and our proper orientation to God)
- *discipleship* (following Christ, biblical themes and stories, prayer and discerning God's will, and the example of prophets and saints)
- *community* (Christian love and responsibilities, ministry, communal support of those in need, religious and moral dialogue, specific moral issues, social justice, church teaching and leadership, worship and preaching, and the religious and moral education of children)

On knowing right from wrong, moral theology often borrows much from moral philosophy.

(Q4) Should believers and nonbelievers come to different conclusions on moral issues?

Believers and nonbelievers should mostly come to the same moral beliefs, for example, that stealing is wrong. But there may be differences. Believers will recognize a duty to worship God while nonbelievers won't. And the two may differ on issues like mercy killing, based on having different beliefs about the origin and destiny of our lives.

I wrote a review (Gensler 1999) on a book by Peter Singer about Henry Spira, who was an important animal-rights activist. Both were very morally committed atheists. At the end of his life, Spira got very sick and committed suicide to avoid a painful death. This makes sense to me if I consider it from an *atheistic* perspective. From a *theistic* perspective, killing God's prized possession at this point makes no sense; how we die is precious, because death is the transition between our earthly life and life with God. A painful death endured with faith, hope, and love can purify us as we prepare to meet God. For believers, how we die is very important; to grasp this difference further, do a Web search for "prayers for a happy death." I should add that, for believers, *every* life is worth living; this makes a difference to beginning-of-life issues too.

(Q5) What advantages does theistic ethics have?

Morality is based on our rational-biological-spiritual nature. Atheists can accept the first two, but not the third.

Believers and nonbelievers share much on morality. Both groups can agree about practical reason – including the importance of being informed, imaginative, and consistent (GR, ends-means, etc.). Both groups can agree on how morality relates to our biological nature – including how we evolved concern for others and a sense of right and wrong; how humans ought to respect possessions, speech, life, and family; and how to use practical reason to explore ethical controversies. And both groups can be deeply committed to morality and can work together to help make the world a better place.

But nonbelievers miss much of the story. Theistic ethics can be more powerful because it appeals to the whole person:

- Morality fits well into our larger theistic picture of reality, since the ultimate explanation of our existence is personal and moral. We were created by a loving and good God. Our lives have a God-given meaning and purpose, that through our moral struggles we may grow in love and wisdom toward our ultimate destiny of eternal life with God. Through our moral struggles, God forms us into the kind of being who can more deeply enjoy him for all eternity.
- We are moral beings (with a knowledge of right and wrong and a free will to choose between the two) because of how God made us. God created us through an evolutionary process that he set up for his own purposes.
- We have greater reason to trust human reason, which God gave us to help us to find truth and to guide our lives. Human reason isn't just from genetic variations that promote jungle survival, without regard for higher goals like truth. So faith in God can enhance our trust in reason.
- We have additional ways to know moral truths; we can know moral truths through reason or through revelation.

- We have additional motives to be moral, including loving gratitude to God, a desire to become more like him, love for his creatures, and the desire for eternal life.
- We have additional resources to be moral, especially prayer and worship, our religious community, the Bible, and the example of Jesus and the saints. For believers, ethics and religion are often tightly interwoven.
- Morality for us is more personal, since it's tied to our personal relationship to God (which includes ups and downs, and God's mercy and forgiveness). The biggest punishment from wrongdoing is that we alienate ourselves from God.
- Morality for us tends to be more objective and more connected with our larger picture of reality, and so it tends to be a more powerful force in our lives (§7.2).
- For us, morality is part of loving God. That's the biggest difference that theism makes to morality.

Nonbelievers, who think that humans are accidents in a universe with no ultimate moral meaning or purpose, by contrast have an impoverished morality. They may have moral feelings and know how to reason about right and wrong, but they lack the context that gives morality a deeper meaning and purpose. Theistic morality is so much richer on a human level.

In addition, theism brings advantages to ethical theory. Theism better explains how ethics can be *well defined* (in that controversial moral questions can have a right answer) and thus more *objective*; and this holds for moral realists (§6.4) and nonrealists (§3.4). Theism better explains the *authority* of moral judgments (§6.5.1). Theism better insures that the moral life requires *no ultimate sacrifice* of our deepest personal interests; we all win by being moral. And theism better supports our hope that, in the final account, *good shall conquer over evil*.

Atheists may respond that this is all fine, except that belief in God has zero evidence. I'll argue later (§§8.5–6) that belief in God has considerable evidence and is very reasonable.

(Q6) You say "meaning or purpose." How do these differ?

As the purpose of a paper-cutter is to cut paper, so too the purpose of a human being is to love God above all things and our neighbor as ourselves, both in this life and the next. This is why we were created, the purpose given to us by our maker. We may also have our own purposes for our lives – for example, to love God and neighbor through our study of philosophy.

I take "meaning" to be broader, to include "purpose" but also the questions in the title of Paul Gauguin's post-Impressionist painting: "Where do we come from? What are we? Where are we going?" Let's compare theistic/atheistic answers to these questions and to the question about purpose:

- *Where do we come from?* A loving and good God created us through a long evolutionary process. / We came into existence through evolution, and behind this process there's no great mind or underlying moral purposes.
- *What are we?* We are God's creatures made in his image and likeness, with rational, biological, and spiritual dimensions. / We are an advanced primate species.
- *What is our ultimate purpose?* We were created to love God and neighbor, in this life and the next. / Human beings as such have no purpose, although individuals can have their own purposes for their lives.
- *Where are we going?* Our ultimate destiny is eternal life with God, and we prepare for this by leading lives of wisdom and love. / When I die I shall rot, and nothing of my ego will survive (Bertrand Russell 1957: 54).

The theistic picture of reality is much friendlier toward values; this makes a big difference in how we look at ethics and at life.

6.6 Interfaith Addendum

Before moving to our final two chapters, I want to discuss something that don't connect closely to the rest of this present chapter. That's why I call this section an "addendum."

My addendum is about *our duties toward those who have a different perspective on faith* – which connects to our ethics-and-religion theme. "Perspective on faith" here covers the range of options that we have about religion, including

- religious faiths (Christian, Muslim, Hindu, Buddhist, Sikh, etc.) and subdivisions of these (Catholic, Protestant, Baptist, Sunni, Shiite, etc.)
- negative perspectives (atheist, agnostic, etc.)

So I take being Christian or Muslim or atheist or agnostic to be a perspective on faith.

Interfaith duties (duties toward those of other perspectives on faith) are especially important today, because our communities have such a pluralistic religious mix and because our world is threatened by hatred, terrorism, and war between those of differing perspectives. How can diverse people learn to live together? The answer is that, despite some sharp differences (e.g., about arranged marriages), good people from diverse groups tend to have some deep values in common. One shared value is GR, which is common to practically every culture and religion. Insofar as we agree on GR and put this agreement into practice, we have a good chance to learn to live together harmoniously.

I suggest that we base *interfaith duties* on GR: that we try to treat another's perspective on faith as we'd want our own to be treated. I want people, when they approach my Christian faith, to[9]

- listen carefully, be fair, show respect, and not distort
- not generalize from a few bad cases (don't say that *all* Christians are evil just because a *few* are)
- not compare the best of their faith with the worst of mine
- give Christianity the benefit of the doubt (so don't take a passage like Luke 14:26, "Unless you hate your father and mother you cannot be my disciple," literally when most Christians don't take it that way)
- neither deny nor exaggerate differences between their faith and mine

We likewise need to treat other perspectives on faith fairly.

Also important is *freedom of religion* – our right to choose which religion (if any) to accept and live by – without persecution, threats, or intimidation. We need to allow others the same freedom of religion that we want for ourselves.

Religion can be divisive. A few years ago, a Christian pastor was planning a "burn a Qur'an" day. Would he want Muslims to plan a "burn a Bible" day? Yes, good people from diverse groups share some deep values. But less enlightened people from diverse groups share some deep disvalues, like divisiveness and stereotypes. Those who spread division are much the same, whether they be Christian, Muslim, Jewish, or atheist.

---

[9] Christian Troll (2008) (a Christian and Jesuit) and Sohaib Saeed (2010) (a Muslim) both apply GR to how we ought to treat those of faith perspectives that differ from our own.

Each perspective on faith needs to use its own resources (including GR) to spread understanding and fair treatment toward those of other perspectives.[10] Religious divisiveness hurts our world (often leading to bloodshed) and keeps us from dealing with common problems (like peace and climate change). We need understanding between different perspectives on faith.

Why did God create a world that has brought forth such a great variety of approaches to religion and supernatural beliefs? Does this somehow serve God's purposes? People say things like the following:

- There are many paths to God.
- Humans struggle to express the object of their search.
- Humans have many ways (all incomplete) to picture God.
- God is too big to fit into one religion.

There's likely some truth in these statements. The Qur'an (5:48) makes another suggestion, that God made us of different faiths to compete with each other in doing good.

But shouldn't a good Catholic, like myself, say that there's only *one true religion* and that all other religions are *false* (and evil)? Not at all![11] The unit of truth is the proposition. As a good Catholic, I hold that all propositions essential to Catholicism are true. In doing this, I also hold

---

[10] Christians should emphasize that Jesus lived in an interfaith world and was positive toward those of other faiths. Those of other faiths portrayed positively in the Gospels include the Wise Men from the East (perhaps Hindus or Zoroastrians), the Roman centurion whose servant Jesus cured, the demented Gentile who lived among the pig-raisers, the Ninivites who reformed their lives after Jonah confronted them, the queen of the South who visited Solomon, the Canaanite woman, Pilate's wife, the Roman centurion at Jesus's death, the Gentile widow that Elias visited, Naaman the Syrian leper who was cured, the Samaritan leper who was cured and gave thanks, and the Good Samaritan who helped a stranger of another faith. All are praised or presented positively. Remember too that Jesus taught us to love everyone.

[11] Vatican II (1962–65) spoke positively about other religions. *Nostra Aetate* 2 says, "The Catholic Church rejects nothing that is true and holy in these religions. She regards with sincere reverence those ways of conduct and of life, those precepts and teachings which, though differing in many aspects from the ones she holds and sets forth, nonetheless often reflect a ray of that Truth which enlightens all men." *Lumen Gentium* 16 says, "Those also can attain to salvation who through no fault of their own do not know the Gospel of Christ or His Church, yet sincerely seek God and moved by grace strive by their deeds to do His will as it is known to them through the dictates of conscience. Nor does Divine Providence deny the helps necessary for salvation to those who, without blame on their part, have not yet arrived at an explicit knowledge of God and with His grace strive to live a good life."

that many beliefs of other religions (especially theistic ones like Judaism, Islam, and Bahá'í) are also true – for religions overlap much in their message. So if I hold that Catholicism's beliefs are true, then I have to hold that large chunks of other faiths are true too.

PART III

ETHICS AND ATHEISM

7

Ethics without God

Our final two chapters are about *ethics and atheism*. Chapter 7 considers how atheists raise ethical objections to religion and how they view ethics. We'll begin with Bertrand Russell; I picked him because of his philosophical stature and strong opposition to religion. Chapter 8 responds to objections.

When I discuss nonbelievers, I have in mind Western-style atheists and agnostics with a scientific worldview; I'm not thinking of traditional Buddhists (who accept reincarnation but no God), or polytheists. I assume traditional definitions of "theist," "atheist," and "agnostic":

- A *theist* is one who believes that there's a God. "God" here means roughly what Copleston and Russell (1948: 390) agreed to in their radio debate: "a supreme personal being – distinct from the world and creator of the world." This belief that there's a God may be seen as certain or uncertain, as backed up by firm argument or not so backed up.
- An *atheist* is one who believes that there's no God. Again, this belief may be seen as certain or uncertain, as backed up by firm argument or not so backed up.
- An *agnostic* is one who takes no stand on whether there's a God. So agnostics are undecided about God.

Another usage sees a *theist* as one who thinks the evidence conclusive that there's a God, an *atheist* as one who thinks the evidence conclusive that there's no God, and an *agnostic* as one who sees the evidence as inconclusive. I dislike this usage because it strangely takes fideists to be *agnostics* if they firmly accept God on faith despite inconclusive evidence.

This "ethics without God" chapter focuses on atheists; but most of what I say also applies to agnostics. For some nonbelievers, the atheist/agnostic distinction isn't important; Russell variously called himself "atheist" or "agnostic."[1]

7.1 Bertrand Russell

Bertrand Russell (1872–1970), one of the most important philosophers of the twentieth century, was born into an aristocratic British family. He lost his parents as a toddler; his grandmother raised him Christian. He struggled with faith as a teenager; he rejected free will and the afterlife but for a time continued to accept God as first cause. At age eighteen, he rejected belief in God upon reading Mill's objection to the first-cause argument (§7.2.1); he remained a nonbeliever for the rest of his life. He rejected belief in God on intellectual and moral grounds.

Russell's intellectual objection was that religion lacked evidence and was discredited by science. First, Russell contended that there was no evidence for God. We just saw that he rejected the first-cause argument. He also criticized other theistic arguments, including the natural-law argument that sees scientific laws as requiring a lawgiver; the design argument (which astonishingly supposes, he says, that this world is the best that omnipotence and omniscience could produce); moral arguments (some of which falter on the Euthyphro question while others groundlessly posit a just God who brings justice to this unjust world); and the ontological argument (which he criticized using his logical theory of denoting; Russell 1905: 491).

Russell also saw science as destroying religion's credibility. Science reveals a world that's godless and lacks meaning and purpose. According to science, the world always existed; and so there's no reason to posit a cause that brought the world into existence. The immensity of the cosmos (including the huge number of stars and planets) shows that intelligent life would likely have evolved somewhere, from random variation and survival of the fittest, and that humanity has no special place in this purposeless world. Our death will end our existence, and the sun's burning out will end humanity.

---

[1] But for atheists moving toward belief, an agnostic "*Maybe* there's a God" can be a big step. For example, see Jennifer Fulwiler (2014: 72); her book is a delightful account of a conversion from atheism to Catholicism.

Religion, which teaches that we were created by a God who helps and protects us, is accepted without evidence because it comforts us in a fearful world. But this make-believe story clashes with science. Adult minds ought to accept beliefs on scientific evidence, instead of on emotions and fantasy.

Russell's moral objection was that religion was harmful:

- Religion, coming from a primitive barbaric age, promotes cruelties that modern consciences reject. So the Old Testament told the Jews to exterminate conquered peoples completely, including women, children, and animals.
- Religion pushes people to believe groundless dogmas, be closed minded, and persecute dissenters. So it poisons the intellect, divides society, and opposes scientific progress.
- Religion teaches an individualistic morality that neglects social consequences. So it brings guilt about healthy sex. And an adulterer who finds a cure for a disease is seen as morally worse than a sexually faithful husband who's so negligent that his children die from preventable diseases.
- The stronger faith is, the stronger is its dogmatism and cruelty; recall witch burnings and Inquisition tortures. If religion today is more moderate, this is only because of influence from freethinkers.

Russell saw religion as a disease born of fear and as a source of misery. It benefited humanity in only two ways: in fixing the calendar and in studying eclipses; it had no other benefits. He also raised the problem of evil: the world has so much suffering that God, if he existed, would have to be a moral monster.

Russell admitted that Christ had some good ideas – like giving our goods to the poor, being nonviolent, and not punishing adulterers; but the Church ignores these and promotes its own power. Christ wasn't as virtuous and wise as Socrates, since he preached damnation for his opponents, told his disciples to hate their parents, cursed the unproductive fig tree, and believed that his second coming would happen soon.

Russell thought we were heading toward a golden age, based on knowledge and universal concern. But first we need to slay the dragon that opposes this, and this dragon is religion.

Russell fiercely attacked religion. Other militant atheists have become popular, including Richard Dawkins, Daniel Dennett, Sam Harris, and Christopher Hutchens – Haught (2008) has a critique; these "new atheists" carry on Russell's objections (and sarcasm) but add little that's new.

They all sound like the third-century pagan Caecilius, who objected that a good God wouldn't create a world with evil, the world can be explained without God, and Christianity is a very negative force in the world (Swindal 2005: 63–70).

7.2 Objections to Religion

I'll divide objections to religion into three groups:

1. *unfair objections* (distortions, for example)
2. *useful warnings* (where believers need to be careful)
3. *genuine issues* (where a longer response is needed)

Russell's objections are often *unfair*. Russell presents himself as the voice of reason, in opposition to unreason (religion). But he continually twists religion to make his case, as do the new atheists. I'll give four examples.

(1) Russell (1957: 6–7) objected to the first-cause argument:

> If everything must have a cause, then God must have a cause. If there can be anything without a cause, it may just as well be the world as God, so there cannot be any validity in that [first-cause] argument.

While atheists often object this way, most classic forms of the first-cause argument, except perhaps ones by college freshmen, don't assume "Everything has a cause." I'd express Aquinas's causal argument (1274: I, q. 2, a. 3) as follows:

> Some things are caused to exist.
> Whatever is caused to exist is caused by something else.
> There's no infinite chain of causes-and-effects.
> If these are true, then there's a first cause (something that causes other
>   things to exist while nothing caused it to exist).
> If there's a first cause, then there's a God.
> ∴ There's a God.

While this has questionable steps, it's far superior to this:

> *Everything has a cause.*
> ∴ The world has a cause.
> If the world has a cause, then there's a God.
> ∴ There's a God.

The italicized premise here just as quickly leads to atheism:

> If there's a God, then there's something (God) with no cause.
> *Everything has a cause.*
> ∴ There's no God.

So Russell attacks a weak form of the argument instead of stronger forms used by believers; he often does this. In criticizing another's arguments, we should consider the strongest forms we can find – not the weakest forms – and we shouldn't present the weakest forms as if they were the strongest forms. Otherwise, we're distorting the case.

(2) Russell contends that science shows that the world is godless and that humanity is an accident in a meaningless universe. Actually, science shows no such thing. "There's no God" and "Humanity is an accident in a meaningless universe" aren't empirical claims that can be tested scientifically. Evolution can be given either an atheist or a believer interpretation:

A. Evolution brought about humans, and there's no God.
B. Evolution brought about humans, and God brought about evolution in order to bring about humans.

If Russell thinks that science (or something else) favors A over B, he needs to say how. In fact, *Russell doesn't even mention B*, even though it's the default view among educated Christians, many of whom are scientists (§§8.6–7 argues for B over A).[2] Again, Russell twists theism to make it look bad.

(3) Russell and many other unbelievers (like Freud 1927) think *we ought not to believe unless there's strong evidence and we ought not to believe on the basis of our feelings*. So theists, who believe in God on the basis of their feelings without strong evidence, violate important rationality duties.

William James (1896: 1–31) and others have raised strong objections to this *ethics of belief*:

• Does Russell's view about needing strong evidence itself have strong evidence? If not, then it ought to be rejected on its own terms. "*Every unproved faith ought to be rejected*" likewise is an unproved faith prescribing its own rejection.
• Russell demands strong evidence from *fear* of being wrong. So he inconsistently accepts his view on emotional grounds.

---

[2] Most educated Christians don't take literally Genesis's creation account, which has *two stories* with conflicting details (1:1–2:3 and 2:4–25: did animals or humans come first?); both teach that God created the world. Arguments against biblical fundamentalism go back at least to Origen (c. 185–254) and were continued by figures like Augustine (354–430) and Galileo; this refutes the myth that Christian thinkers were all fundamentalists before the rise of modern science. For texts, see Swindal (2005: 7–8, 75–76, 101, 241–44). The "new atheists" also take fundamentalism as their target, largely ignoring more sophisticated forms of theism.

- Imagine a lost woman who believes on weak evidence *that she'll find her way out* – which then becomes true because she believed it. Russell's view absurdly forbids such belief.
- In many areas (such as whom to befriend, marry, or vote for), we need to act on inconclusive evidence. Almost all of us form such beliefs as best we can, on weaker evidence. So Russell's view condemns our almost universal practice.
- For many central beliefs (for example, that we should trust that our senses reveal an external world), we lack strong evidence; but our passionate nature pushes us to believe. Russell's view would paralyze us by forbidding such beliefs.
- We all have opinions based on weak evidence, for example, that tomorrow will be sunny and that Michigan will win. Despite Russell, such opinions doesn't corrupt the mind.
- Science makes more progress if opposing sides on controversial issues adopt and investigate beliefs based on hunches – instead of remaining neutral until we get firm evidence.
- Knowers have two norms: "Know the truth" and "Avoid error" (§4.2.4). Russell is unbalanced on the skeptical side. Russell fears error; but we should also fear that overly high standards may keep us from gaining truths.

In contrast, William James affirmed our right to follow our feelings on important issues (like God and free will) that can't be decided on purely intellectual grounds.[3]

Russell and others simply assume a controversial view on the *ethics of belief* (that we ought never to believe on our feelings without strong evidence) *without even mentioning strong and well-known objections.* This is unfair. If we assume a view to which there are strong objections, we should mention and deal with the objections. Otherwise, we mislead people into thinking that our argument is much stronger than it actually is.

(4) Russell ignores his skeptical norms when he considers religion's social value. Here he firmly believes on flimsy evidence the very worst: *that religion has been almost totally negative and has benefited humanity in only two minor areas* (calendars and eclipses).[4] This claim is really

---

[3] I'll later show that we *can* make a strong case for God's existence (§§8.5–6). But even if this fails, I'd hold that we have a right to believe on the basis of our feelings, so long as there's no disproof of God's existence.

[4] Russell (1957: 26). The new atheists say similar things; Christopher Hitchens wrote a book subtitled *How Religion Poisons Everything.*

absurd; the slightest research would have showed its absurdity. Let me mention just a few other ways that religion has benefited humanity.

Religion has contributed much to education. Cambridge, where Russell studied, had a religious origin, and many of its colleges have religious names (like Jesus, Corpus Christi, Trinity, and St. John's). Many other fine schools at every level have religious connections, and these are generally open to students of every religious perspective. Religion has promoted charitable works (like hospitals, orphanages, hospices, soup kitchens, and shelters for battered women) and help for people with special needs (like alcoholics, the bereaved, immigrants who need to learn English, and couples about to get married). Religion has promoted great art (including paintings, architecture, and music) and moral heroes (like Martin Luther King, Mahatma Gandhi, Nelson Mandela, and Mother Teresa). Religion gave birth to modern science and taught the world a universalist ethics. And religion has enhanced the lives of countless people, in terms of joy, benevolence, and the meaningfulness of life.

And yet Russell couldn't find ways that religion benefited humanity (apart from calendars and eclipses). He could have found many such ways had he looked. Russell condemned believing without strong evidence; but he didn't apply this to believing bad things about your opponents, where flimsy evidence suffices. Does anyone detect the inconsistency?

Every racial, ethnic, and religious group has good and bad. It's bigotry to see only good on your side and bad on the other. By this measure, Russell was a religious bigot, not the voice of reason.

Russell's daughter, Kate Tait, was raised atheist but later became Christian. Her book (1975: 94, 180–91) complains that Russell (and the school he founded) never presented religion fairly. Russell's religious upbringing was negative, making high moral demands and filling him with guilt when he fell short; he continued a secular version of this after rejecting God. But Tait found joy in believing that God loves and forgives us.

Parents need to respect their offsprings' right to make their own choices about religion. Russell tried to do this, and he even financed Tait's husband's training to become a minister.

Unbelievers are often unfair toward believers, and believers are often unfair toward nonbelievers. A book on *ethics and religion* should condemn this. Unfairness toward other perspectives on religion is bad for at least three reasons.

First, it violates the golden rule (§6.6). We ought to treat the perspective on faith of another as we want our own to be treated: with fairness, without distortion, not seeing just their negatives and our positives, and so on.

Second, such unfairness blocks progress. The God-question is difficult. People on both sides are frail humans, pursuing one of life's big questions. We need to work together: I pursue the God-view, you pursue the no-God-view, and we both try to find weaknesses in the other's position; this pushes us to develop our thinking. Such cooperation promotes good science and good philosophy; it's unproductive to just distort each other's views. Atheists who criticize religion need to follow J. L. Mackie (who argued fairly) instead of Russell and the new atheists.

Third, such unfairness inhibits moral cooperation. People of all perspectives on faith need to work together to deal with common problems, like war and global warming. Unfairness toward other perspectives divides people and discourages cooperation.

Some atheistic objections are *useful warnings* about areas where believers need to be more careful.

When I read militant atheists, I see stereotypes about what believers are like: antiscience, authoritarian, blindly obedient, narrow minded, fundamentalist, intolerant, judgmental, antigay, racist, guilt ridden, and hypocritical; they act morally only to avoid hell, hate those of other faiths, think they're better than other people, and try to force their beliefs on others.[5]

Most Christians that I know aren't like this; they're tolerant, pro-science, nonfundamentalist, and so forth. But *some* Christians have some of these bad features. Some may even follow a perverted Christianity that hates its neighbor. Frederick Douglass (1855: 151), an ex-slave who experienced perverted religion, distinguished good from bad forms of Christianity:

> I love the religion of our blessed Savior.... I love that religion that is based upon the glorious principle, of love to God and love to man; which makes its followers do unto others as they themselves would be done by. If you demand liberty to yourself, it says, grant it to your neighbors. If you claim a right to think for yourself, allow your neighbors the same right.... It is because I love this

---

[5] Atheists suffer from stereotypes too. They're sometimes seen as amoral, relativistic, selfish, dogmatic, untrustworthy, evil, bitter, disrespectful, and angry; they worship science, criticize what they don't understand, have meaningless lives, and would love to persecute believers (as did many Marxist atheists). Both sides need to move away from stereotypes. I myself find most atheists to be honest people with high standards of evidence.

religion that I hate the slaveholding, the woman-whipping, the mind-darkening, the soul-destroying religion that exists in the southern states of America.

Jesus also criticized a perverted religion of mechanical rules and hatred toward enemies and sinners; he instead taught forgiveness, loving enemies, and being guided by a loving God.[6]

When we read those who say that religion is evil, we have a right to protest the stereotypes. But we must admit that *perverted religion can be very evil*. And we can take the stereotypes as a warning about how religion can be perverted.

Some atheistic objections are *genuine issues* that demand a longer response. These two are especially important: (1) "How can we believe that a good God created a world with so much evil?" and (2) "Since science explains the world, why do we need God?" Chapter 8 discusses these two.

As an antidote to Russell's negativity toward religion, I recommend Bruce Sheiman's (2009) *An Atheist Defends Religion: Why Humanity Is Better Off with Religion Than without It*. Its introduction claims, "By any empirical measure – defined in terms of theism's practical impact on individuals, society, and culture – religion is profoundly beneficial." Sheiman claims that strong empirical evidence shows that religious people, while accepting much the same moral norms as nonbelievers, tend to live out their morality better and be healthier and happier. Believers come out better by practically any measure: charitable giving, volunteering, donating blood, depression rates, suicide attempts, drug addiction, divorces, exercise, heart attacks, criminality, longevity, marital satisfaction, self-acceptance, moral purpose, peacefulness, personal happiness, and so on.[7] Sheiman sees religion as securing moral standards, teaching moral objectivity and universal love, and being the strongest force for morality and personal happiness. He claims that militant atheists who see religion as very harmful ignore massive empirical data to the contrary. And yet, he's

---

[6] The *genuine / perverted religion* distinction cuts across faith boundaries. So there are those who stress love (or hate) in Christianity, Islam, Judaism, Hinduism, and so on. Those who stress love often feel a closer bond with loving members of other faiths than toward hating members of their own faith.

[7] See also Glynn (1997: 57–97), who mentions many further studies, and Iannaccone (1998), who mentions studies disputing the myth that religion is gradually disappearing as people become more educated and scientific.

an atheist; while seeing the tremendous value of religion, he cannot accept it himself.

7.3 Atheist Ethics Options

Atheists can hold *any* approach to ethics, even ones that affirm morality's objectivity or its dependence on God. Bertrand Russell, for example, held various views about ethics:

- *Intuitionism (nonnaturalism)*: He first saw ethics as objective and based on intuited first principles (along the lines of his fellow unbeliever G. E. Moore). Basic moral terms are indefinable, and independent moral facts determine the truth or falsity of moral judgments.
- *Error theory*: He later held (with the atheist J. L. Mackie) that moral judgments make objective claims but are all false – since there are no moral facts.
- *Emotivism*: He sometimes held (with the atheist A. J. Ayer) that moral judgments express emotional exclamations instead of truths claims: "A is intrinsically good" means "Would that everyone desire A!"
- *Confusion*: He finally admitted unclarity about ethics and dissatisfaction with his previous views.[8]

Other ethical approaches that atheists could take include the following:

- *Naturalism about moral concepts*: "Good" is definable in descriptive, empirical terms (as perhaps "socially accepted," "what I like," "what accords with evolution," or "what an ideal observer would prescribe"). So moral judgments are true-or-false empirical descriptions of the world.
- *Naturalism about moral properties*: While *moral concepts* aren't definable, *moral properties* are ordinary empirical properties – so the property of being a good action may be identical to the property of being socially accepted. Again, moral judgments are true-or-false empirical descriptions.
- *Moderate emotivism*: Moral judgments, while expressing emotions, can be rationally appraised; *rational ethical feelings* are ones that are informed, impartial, consistent, and so forth. We'd agree on most or

---

[8] Russell's moral critique presupposes that religion has *objectively* bad consequences and that any Creator of this suffering world would be *objectively* evil. In their debate, Copleston complained that Russell's dismissive comments, like "'Ought'... is an echo of what one has been told by one's parents," clash with his strong moral stands (Copleston and Russell 1948: 397–98).

all of our moral beliefs if we were rational; this leads to a degree of moral objectivity.

• *Universal prescriptivism*: Moral judgments are imperatives (like "Do this") that apply to all similar cases; this leads to a golden-rule consistency condition: I can't consistently hold that I ought to do A to X unless I also prescribe that, if I were in X's exact place, then A be done to me. We'd agree on most or all of our moral beliefs if we were rational (consistent, informed, and imaginative); this leads to a high degree of moral objectivity.

Such approaches are open to believers and nonbelievers and are usually presented with little or no mention of God. And so most atheists think that morality can do fine without God.[9]

Atheists also could accept divine-command views that see objective duties as requiring God (§2.7.1). Indeed, some prominent atheists (including Frederick Nietzsche, Jean-Paul Sartre, Simone de Beauvoir, and some of Dostoevsky's fictional characters) insist that *if God doesn't exist, then everything is permitted*. They'd add that, since God *doesn't* exist, therefore everything *is* permitted. Such atheists reject all duties (or sometimes just all objective duties).

If I were an atheist, I'd adopt a view that makes ethics as objective and rational as possible. If I were an *atheist who rejected strong moral realism*, I'd hold the view from Chapter 3 (§3.6), which proposes that we take "good action" to mean "action desired by the highest available wisdom and love." Atheists would add that, since there's no God, the highest available wisdom and love is *human wisdom and love*. This gives a somewhat acceptable ethics, even though it leaves ethics poorly defined (since idealized human wisdom and love can disagree; §3.4). If I were an *atheist who accepted strong moral realism*, I'd hold the natural-law view from Chapters 5 and 6 (about practical reason and its application to *Homo sapiens*), but I'd reject the spirituality of Chapter 7. This pared-down NL view also gives a somewhat acceptable atheistic ethics, even though the theistic version has many advantages.

Atheists have a wider range of philosophical options than believers. Imagine an essay that begins, "Science is the only way of knowing, only matter exists, free will is an illusion, and ethics is just about feelings." The author

---

[9] For more on these approaches, see §2.5, §3.7, Gensler (2011a), and Gensler and Spurgin (2008). I don't claim that my list is exhaustive or that all these views are plausible (Gensler 2011a attacks most of them). Evans (2013: 118–54) and Ritchie (2012: 67–157) criticize several atheistic approaches to ethics.

isn't likely to be a believer; it would be difficult to believe in God while believing such things.

Suppose we believe, with the theistic world religions, in one supreme personal God who created the world out of love for us and revealed himself and his will through sacred writings. However we may see morality philosophically, we also see it as God's will for us. God created us with the ability to know right from wrong and to choose. The most important norms are love of God and neighbor, and the golden rule. Morality is serious, objective, and part of our personal relationship toward God. Right living can have religious motives, both higher (unselfish love and gratitude) and lower (punishments and rewards), and moves us toward our destiny of eternal happiness with God.

Philosophical views like the following are congenial to genuine religion (with their opposites being uncongenial):

- Morality is objective (God wouldn't command mere social conventions or individual feelings), knowable because of how God made us, and requires concern for everyone.
- We have free will (or else the evil we do would be caused by God and we wouldn't be responsible for it).[10]
- Our knowledge and reasonable belief aren't limited to what is scientifically provable (since belief in God is reasonable).
- There's life after death and our ultimate purpose involves eternal life with God; so humans aren't completely explainable in material terms.

So religious philosophers tend to share certain beliefs and thus have definite *family resemblances*. Theistic philosophers need to defend views congenial to theism.[11]

Most thinkers try to keep their ideas consistent with *science* and *common sense*. Religious thinkers see *religion* as another constraint. I see all three as helping to keep us from error.

Atheistic philosophers, being unconstrained by religion, can hold a wider range of views on the points mentioned previously:

---

[10] Luther and Calvin rejected free will, seeing it as threatening God's absolute control over the universe. But contemporary Lutherans and Calvinists tend to accept free will as important for Christianity.

[11] See Plantinga (1983). Some philosophical views (like early Augustine's view that only material objects exist – see Swindal 2005: 87–88) can impede belief; questioning these can be a big step toward conversion.

- Atheists can affirm or deny the objectivity of morality;[12] and they can accept an altruistic or an egoistic morality.
- Atheists can affirm or deny free will or accept a weak compatibilist free will.
- Atheists can affirm or deny that our knowledge is limited to what's scientifically provable.
- Atheists can affirm or deny that there's life after death[13] and that humans are completely explainable in material terms.

Atheists also differ among themselves in further ways:

- Some atheists make a big deal of their atheism, while others scarcely mention it.
- Some atheists emphasize the absurdity of our existence, while others talk about how our individual concerns and projects can give meaning to our lives.
- Some atheists see the rejection of religion as a liberation, while others see it as a deeply emotional loss that they endure for the sake of intellectual integrity.
- Some atheists, like Russell, are unfair toward religion, distorting it and seeing only its negative aspects. But most atheists try to be fair.
- Some atheists are obsessed about religion and God, while others give these little thought.

So atheistic philosophers, apart from rejecting God, have few family resemblances.

Many atheistic thinkers, however, have a special interest in evolution, which plausibly explains how humans could emerge without being directly created by God. Many try to connect evolution with ethics. There are three main options.

(Option 1) *Evolution gives the foundation for an objective ethics.* The clearest form of this, *ethical evolutionism*, takes "X is good" to mean

---

[12] Judging from a recent survey (Bourget and Chalmers 2014: 476), most professional philosophers accept or lean toward moral realism (56 percent), and most accept or lean toward atheism (73 percent). (Professors tend to be more skeptical about religion than the general public.) So we can suppose that a substantial number of atheistic philosophers affirm the objectivity of morality.

[13] A few atheists accept life after death. A. J. Ayer (1988) had a vivid near-death experience, apparently seeing a bright red light that governed the universe; this weakened his rejection of the afterlife more than his atheism. He mentioned several atheists who viewed the afterlife as certain or possible.

"X accords with the main current of evolution." On this view, moral norms can be deduced from scientific facts about evolution. While popular just after Darwin, this view is unpopular today – for three reasons.

(1a) The *descriptive* "more evolved" differs from the *evaluative* "good." If something is *more evolved*, it's a further question whether it's *good*. Suppose that evolution moves toward increased misery; would it follow that promoting misery is good? Surely not. Depending on what the path of evolution is, supporting it could be either good or bad. Similarly, if evolution put various inclinations into us, we'd still need to ask which of these we ought to follow and which we ought to resist.

(1b) Ethical evolutionism makes no sense from a natural history perspective. If "X is good" means "X accords with the main current of evolution," then how could anyone who lived before Darwin make moral judgments?

(1c) Evolution's "main current" is disputed. *Social Darwinists* see evolution as a dog-eat-dog struggle where the strong survive and crush the weak. Human life does and ought to follow the same pattern; so it's natural and right that strong individuals, businesses, social classes, and races crush the weak. But Darwin himself and many others see humans as social animals that survive because they evolved an instinctual cooperation and caring about each other – first for members of their own clan and then later, with cultural evolution, for all humanity. Darwin summed up this higher morality in the golden rule, "Treat others as you want to be treated."[14]

(Option 2) *Evolution leads to skepticism about ethics.* This view is based on evolutionary explanations of morality. Ruse (1986: 253) says that "morality is a collective illusion foisted upon us by our genes," and Joyce (2006) holds a similar view.

But suppose that our genes enable us to think ethically; how does this show that ethical thinking is an illusion? Since our genes also enable us to think scientifically, should we be skeptical about science too? Both inferences commit the *genetic fallacy*: they explain why people hold a belief and then, simply from this, dismiss the belief as false or unreasonable.[15]

---

[14] Many Christians, influenced by the French Jesuit Pierre Teilhard de Chardin (see Swindal 2005: 326–29), see evolution as part of a larger cosmic process tending toward greater complexity and consciousness, ending with the growth of humanity in knowledge and love toward the final Kingdom of God (the Omega Point). So love of God and neighbor accords deeply with the cosmic process. Teilhard influenced Vatican II (1962–65), especially *The Church in the Modern World* document, which emphasizes change and speaks of our pilgrimage toward the heavenly city.

[15] Antireligious authors often commit this fallacy. They explain belief in God from our emotional need for an idealized father to protect us; they conclude that belief in God is

Some think evolution should explain everything. But when we use reason to learn about the world, rationality norms come first. Scientific thinking needs norms like "We *ought* normally to believe our sense experience," "We *ought* to be consistent," and "Views are *better* if they're simpler and explain more." Scientific method is based on norms like these. So if science destroys norms, then science destroys science.

(Option 3) *Evolution enhances our understanding of ethics.* On this view, evolution contributes to morality by helping us to better understand human nature and how ethical thinking evolved in early humans. Darwin and I accept this option.[16]

7.4 Atheistic Religion

Some atheists contend that *religions are essentially ethical communities* and would do better to drop supernatural beliefs. This suggests the possibility of atheistic religion.

Rabbi Sherwin Wine (1985), the patron of atheistic religion, rejected God on the basis of logical positivism (which today has been almost universally abandoned; see §5.5.2.1). Valuing his Jewish identity, Wine founded Humanistic Judaism, which celebrates Judaism while dropping God. I heard Rabbi Wine speak when I was an undergraduate in the 1960s (we both are Detroiters). Back then, a few Christian thinkers (like Gianni Vahanian, Thomas Altizer, and Paul Van Buren) were prompting the death-of-God movement (and the April 8, 1966, cover of *Time* magazine asked, "Is God Dead?"); but atheistic Christianity didn't catch on.[17] Today, atheistic religion is well represented by Harvard's Humanistic chaplain, Greg Epstein (2009), and by Unitarian Universalism (McGowan 2013: 139–42).

What is atheistic religion like? Let's look at it from four angles: creed, code, cult, and community.

(1) While God is optional or rejected, atheistic religion may have a minimal *creed* that affirms values like tolerance, honesty, justice, and community.

---

false. But God could use this mechanism to get us to believe in him. Or they explain belief in God by a God-gene that evolution gave us to enhance our survival; they conclude that belief in God is false. But God could use this gene to get us to believe in him. Explanations like father-figure and God-gene are neutral about whether God actually exists.

[16] Gensler (2009b; 2013: 131–35) have more on ethics and evolution.

[17] "God is dead," said Nietzsche. "No, Nietzsche is dead," said God.

(2) Atheistic religion can have a *code* based on "Love your neighbor" or "Treat others as you want to be treated" – and subsidiary principles about tolerance, justice, the dignity of the human person, and helping others in times of need.

(3) Atheistic religion can have a nontheistic *cult* (worship) that celebrates aspects of life, like birth (a naming ceremony instead of a baptism), coming of age (like bar/bat mitzvah or confirmation), marriage, death (where a life is celebrated but no afterlife is mentioned), religious holidays, and weekly worship (which celebrates life and right living).

Nontheistic prayer has a role. We can express appreciation for life's good things (instead of thanking God), express hopes and exhortations (instead of petitioning God), and feel peace in the universe's presence (instead of in God's presence). To grasp this better, I constructed nontheistic forms of the Our Father and the grace before meals:

Our Father is the earth that brought us forth; let's respect it with a deep sense of mystery and awe. As brothers and sisters of this planet, let us promote harmony among all people. May we have food to eat every day. May we forgive others as we ourselves want to be forgiven. And may we be freed from evil and temptation. Amen.

We are appreciative for this food – to the earth and the farmers who grew it, and the cooks who prepared it. May it nourish our bodies and our togetherness, and may we share with those who have less. Amen.

Individual prayer is possible too. We can set aside quiet time to review our day (appreciating good things and regretting failings), reflect on our values and how to put them into action, and quietly appreciate being a child of the universe.

(4) Atheistic religion can form *communities* that celebrate life together, contribute to one's identity (perhaps as members of St. Darwin's Parish), and reach out to help others. Religions often sponsor charities (like hospitals, soup kitchens, shelters for the homeless, and treatment centers for alcoholics; see §7.2.4); now atheists can have their own religious charities.

Atheistic religion can provide communal support for nonbelievers while respecting doubts about God; this is good, as far as it goes. But atheistic religion is a weak substitute for the real thing. Real religion does more than help us be ethical and deal with problems; it also fills our lives with a deep love of God.

In this book, I usually treat religion and God together, as if religion (at least in a modern, Western sense; §1.3) necessarily includes belief in God. But now it seems that things aren't so simple. You can belong to an organized religion or not (being *religious* or *nonreligious*) – and you can believe in God or not (being a *theist* or *nontheist*). These are independent options. So there are four basic combinations; you can be a

religious theist,
religious nontheist,
nonreligious theist, or
nonreligious nontheist.

C. S. Lewis was a *religious theist*; he was Christian by religion and believed in God. Sherwin Wine was a *religious nontheist*; he was Humanistic Jewish by religion and rejected belief in God. Antony Flew after his conversion (§§8.6–7) was a *nonreligious theist*; he belonged to no religion but believed in God. And Bertrand Russell was a *nonreligious nontheist*; he belonged to no religion and rejected belief in God.

Many fit into the "nonreligious theist" category; they believe in God but don't formally belong to any church or religion. Such people may reject divine revelation or the need for institutional religion; sometimes they describe themselves as "spiritual but not religious" or "deists" or "unchurched Christians."[18] So, interestingly enough, some theists "go it alone" and see little value in religious communal support – while some atheists see much value in religious communal support.[19]

7.5 Atheists Do Good

Can atheists contribute in a special way to morality and to God's purposes? How would the world be less good without atheists? My answer is that atheism, at its best, can especially contribute pure motivation, courage and intellectual integrity, moral innovation, and challenge to believers.

(1) *Pure motivation.* Monroe (1990) is a study of thirteen people who risked their lives to help Jews escape from the Nazis; it argues that humans can care about others for their own sake, without self-interested motivation. The rescuers came from various religions and included atheists and agnostics.

---

[18] Those with no church membership have been a big group in American history, covering 83 percent of the population during the American revolution and 66 percent in the mid-1800s, but only 40 percent at the end of the 1900s (Iannaccone 1998: 1468). Today the unchurched are again increasing.

[19] Martin (2010: Chapter 2) nicely describes six ways to seek God: belief, independence, disbelief, return, exploration, and confusion. I'd add apathy.

Atheist rescuers could say, "I want to help these Jews, because they desperately need my help. I realize that my action may bring about my own ultimate misery. Those who believe in God and heaven say that good action is always rewarded; but I cannot accept this. Yes, I help these Jews even though I know that this may ultimately ruin me." Perhaps an heroic atheist with such altruism, despite a worldview that pulls against it, has the higher virtue and greater reward.

(2) *Courage and intellectual integrity.* Many atheists honestly stick with their views even when they know that this will lead to ridicule and even persecution. Such courage and intellectual integrity should be respected and praised.[20]

(3) *Moral innovation.* Many atheists think outside the box on moral matters (for example, Peter Singer and Henry Spira opposed cruel methods of testing cosmetics on animals). While this can lead to error, it can also lead to important insights.

(4) *Challenge to believers.* Atheists can challenge believers on moral and intellectual matters. And their presence can help to make belief in God a deeply personal choice rather than what one does without reflection or struggle. In these ways, atheists can help to promote genuine religion.

I've said that atheism *at its best* contributes good things. *At its worst,* it brings selfishness and moral apathy, wallows in life's absurdity, distorts the views of believers (thus violating intellectual integrity), and persecutes believers (Marxists killed many for their faith). There's good and bad on both sides of the theist/atheist divide.

For believers upset that I'm discussing the good that atheists can do, let me mention a homily by Pope Francis (2013). His Gospel passage was Mark 9:38–40 – intolerant disciples complain about one who does good but doesn't belong to their group. Jesus rebukes them, saying, "Let him do good." The disciples thought they *alone* could do good, because they *alone* had the truth. Francis says this is a grave error and can lead to war and killing in God's name. He says that *everyone* can do good, even atheists, who are also children of God and redeemed by Christ.

Interfaith work focuses on common areas that promote peace and understanding – like the golden rule (see Gensler 2013: esp. Chapters 3

---

[20] Believers also may be ridiculed and persecuted for their beliefs, including student believers at secularized schools. Courage and intellectual integrity need to be respected on both sides.

and 5), which is also very popular among nonbelievers.[21] Across world religions, and also between believers and nonbelievers, ethics is more widely shared than theology. What can most bring believers and nonbelievers together, and promote mutual understanding, is a common commitment to "doing good" (as Pope Francis put it). We need, despite theological differences, to work together to promote peace, justice, mutual understanding, and the health of our planet.

[21] The golden rule is also strong among nonbelievers; for example, Greg Epstein (2009) and Dale McGowan (2013) emphasize it. Robert Romig's (1984) "reasonable religion" drops God but keeps the golden rule.

8

God, Evil, and Cosmic Purpose

St. Thomas Aquinas (1274: I, q. 1, a. 3) gave two objections to belief in
God:

Does God exist? It seems that God does not exist; because if . . . God existed, there
would be no evil discoverable; but there is evil in the world. Therefore God does
not exist.

It is superfluous to suppose that what can be accounted for by a few principles
has been produced by many. But it seems that everything we see in the world can
be accounted for by other principles, supposing God did not exist. . . . Therefore
there is no need to suppose God's existence.

The *problem of evil* and *unnecessary hypothesis* are still the main objections to belief in God. My response emphasizes moral ideas. I'll defend
God's moral goodness, against the *problem of evil*; and I'll argue that
God's moral purposes are part of our best explanation of why the world
exists as it does, against the *unnecessary hypothesis*.

8.1 Why Evil?

With all the evil and suffering in the world, is it reasonable to believe that
a good and perfect God created the world?

I live in Chicago. Here many evils happen every year – deaths, diseases,
poverty, robberies, tornadoes, and so forth – bringing physical pain and
mental suffering. Similar evils take place all over the world. Now imagine
that there's a being X, who either caused these evils or could easily have
prevented them. X had the power to bring only joy to people, if he had so
chosen, but instead brought about (or at least permitted) massive evils.

Here X, of course, is God; Bertrand Russell says that X would be a moral monster if he existed. Should we agree?

Here's a traditional formulation of the problem of evil:

> If God doesn't want to prevent evil, then he isn't all good.
> If God isn't able to prevent evil, then he isn't all powerful.
> Either God doesn't want to prevent evil, or he isn't able.
> ∴ Either God isn't all powerful, or he isn't all good.

The first two premises are based on taking an "all good being" as *one who wants to do good and prevent evil as far as he's able* – and an "all powerful being" as *one who's able to do anything that's logically consistent*. The third premise is based on the argument that if God wanted to prevent evil and was able to do so, then he'd do it and there'd be no evil – which goes against the clear fact that there *is* evil. And the conclusion follows, which requires giving up God or his power or his goodness.[1]

Most theists dispute premise 1, saying that the all-good God has a *reason* for not wanting to prevent evil. Proposed reasons are "theodicies," and we'll look at three popular ones.[2]

Traditional theodicy: In Catholic grade school, I learned that God, who is all-good and all-powerful, created a world with perfect free creatures, Adam and Eve, who sinned. Before sin, the world had no suffering, death, or disease. All evil comes from the abuse of free will, as either a just punishment or a natural consequence. God permits evil because he could prevent it only by taking away our free will, and thus our capacity for moral goodness; this would result in a less-good world.

This traditional theodicy faces problems of four sorts:

- *Scientific*: From an evolutionary view, the first humans would have been immature, just higher than apes, and not perfect. And suffering, death, disease, tornados, and other evils would have existed long before the first humans.
- *Psychological*: A perfect Adam and Eve likely wouldn't have sinned. If they did sin, then God likely created them poorly, tempted them too strongly, or kept them ignorant of what would happen if they sinned.
- *Biblical*: There are reasons, based on inconsistent details in Genesis (e.g., whether animals came before humans), for not taking the creation

---

[1] Some believers respond by claiming that God is all-good but limited in his power to combat evil. While this view is important, I won't discuss it here.

[2] A theodicy is a tool for debating with atheists, not a pastoral tool for helping those in grief. These two tools are often confused.

accounts literally. Why then take the sin and punishment of Adam and Eve literally?

- *Moral*: Why would it be right for God to punish innocent children today (by giving them painful diseases, for example) because of a sin committed by their distant ancestors?

The traditional theodicy is loaded with problems.

Mystery theodicy: Evil is a mystery. We must trust that God has a reason for permitting evil, even though our little minds cannot grasp what this reason is.

This answer is evasive and will provoke scorn from those who use evil to attack belief in God. Those who struggle with faith also need a better answer. Believers need to give *some* answer about why God might permit evil, even if it's incomplete, as all human answers are. Believers need to raise doubts about the problem-of-evil argument, even if we'll never completely understand evil or God's purposes.

Irenaean theodicy: St. Irenaeus (c. 120–200) was a bishop and theologian of the early church; John Hick further developed his suggestions about evil.[3] On Irenaean theodicy, God is all-good and all-powerful. God created a world of imperfect, weak, free beings who, by struggling against evil, can grow in spiritual maturity toward greater faith and love – which will reach perfection only in the afterlife. God permits evil because it's required for the significance of the human epic. Our life is like the way of the cross leading to the resurrection.

Let's now consider and evaluate various possible answers to this question: "Supposing that you were a perfect God, what sort of world would you create?"

(1) "*If I were a perfect God, I'd create the best of all possible worlds.*" But maybe there's no "best" possible world, just as there's no highest number; maybe for each finite world there could be a better one. And maybe any really good world requires free beings whose choices could make the world better or worse; but then these free beings could, and likely would, bring about evil, which would make the world less good.

(2) "*If I were a perfect God, I'd create a world of great enjoyment, knowledge, and love – without suffering, ignorance, or hatred – and our actions couldn't upset this.*" But this wouldn't be very meaningful; our actions wouldn't matter and so would lack significance. And how great is

[3] See Hick (1978) and the Irenaeus and Gensler selections in Swindal (2004: 54–57, 523–31).

"great" here? There seem to be endless degrees of enjoyment, knowledge, and love – mirroring the infinite gap between finite and infinite beings.

(3) *"If I were a perfect God, I'd create a world where free beings can struggle meaningfully and lovingly against evil."* I see the value of this. The news had a story about a divorcee on welfare with three dying children. The woman could give up and drink away her problems – or struggle lovingly to make life bearable for her family. There's a chance for something of great value and beauty in a world where the freedom to love can make a difference. And yet, while we value the free struggle against evil, we also value having evil overcome.

(4) *"If I were a perfect God, I'd create a world with two phases: heroic struggle (this present life) and evil overcome (heaven). Each phase has values lacking in the other; but the two together are complete."* This is Irenaean theodicy. It fits our §6.3 Genesis story, where God chooses *struggle* instead of *easy*:

God decided to share his love and goodness with others, by creating rational creatures in his image and likeness. But how would he create them? God rejected an easy solution: to create rational creatures fully formed and share his life with them. God decided instead that his rational creatures would struggle and grow through free choices, taking a long journey back to him (and to eternal life); he judged that a long, epic struggle toward the final fulfillment would ultimately be more meaningful.

My weaker side regrets God's choice every day, as I complain, "Why is life so hard and painful?" In reflective moments, I see that God picked the better and more meaningful path for us. And from the view of eternity, God's choice wins easily.

8.2 Ethical Theories

The problem of evil uses a *moral premise* ("If God . . ., then he isn't *good*"). So our views about morality may impact how we understand the problem of evil (see Carson 2007).

Suppose that you're an atheist who, based on emotivism or some other theory, rejects objective ethical truths. You can't then use the problem-of-evil argument in the usual way, since you can't hold that its moral premise is objectively *true*.[4] But then you have at least three other alternatives.

---

[4] C. S. Lewis and others claim that any moral premise requires a belief in objective moral truths and thus a belief in God (§2.1). Mackie sidesteps the problem by not asserting the truth of a moral premise but just pointing out inconsistency in the theist's belief system.

(1) J. L. Mackie (1955) avoids asserting premises that would be construed as moral truths. Instead, he argues that theism is *inconsistent* in combining these three beliefs: "God is omnipotent; God is wholly good; and evil exists." Deriving a contradiction, he says, requires two further principles based on the meaning of "omnipotent" and "wholly good." But Alvin Plantinga (1974: 7–64) argued that these further principles are misworded and the correct wording blocks the contradiction. He further argued for the consistency of the three beliefs by showing that all three would be true in a possible situation described by a version on the traditional theodicy. It's widely accepted that Plantinga successfully rebutted Mackie's inconsistency charge.

(2) Antony Flew (1955) also avoided premises that would be construed as moral truths. Instead, he asked believers what experiences would lead them, correctly, to give up "God loves us." To theists who said that no experiences could lead them to reject this, he'd reply that then this belief must be meaningless. This inference is based on a version of the now discredited logical positivism (§5.5.2.1). And believers could respond, "If I saw that God makes us do evil and then severely punishes us for all eternity for doing it, then I'd stop believing that God loves us."

(3) Emotivists could give us alleged facts about how God, if he existed, would have to have been cruel to create this world, hoping that this will lead us to say "Boo on God!" (emotivism's opposite of "God is good") or "God doesn't love us." So several forms of the problem-of-evil objection are available to atheistic philosophers who reject objective moral truths. And believers can defend themselves using Irenaean theodicy.

Traditional divine command theory (Chapter 2) dissolves the problem of evil; if *being good = doing what God desires*, then a cruel God who does what he desires is automatically good. This is implausible; evil *should* be a problem for believers.

Our modified DCT (Chapter 3) bases morality on the will of a wise and loving God. Then the issue becomes whether our world, with its misery, could have been created by a wise and loving God. Irenaean theodicy can argue for a yes answer.

Our natural-law theory in Chapters 4–6 saw humans as subject to moral norms of three sorts: rational, biological, and spiritual. How do these apply to God and the problem of evil?

Spiritual norms: "Love God above all things" may apply to God too, but this doesn't involve the problem of evil.

Biological norms: Among the biological norms applying to humans, those against stealing, lying, killing, and adultery are central (§5.3). Such norms are based on applying practical reason (including GR) to *human nature* and needn't apply to other rational beings. Imagine angels who lack possessions (and so can't steal from each other), already know all truths (and so can't lie to each other), can't die (and so can't kill each other), and aren't sexual (and so can't commit adultery). God too has a very different nature from ours and wouldn't be subject to our biological norms. Can God steal? He owns everything. Can God commit adultery? He isn't sexual. Can God kill? Yes, he eventually kills everyone; but this is needed in our present world to make room for the next generation (Clancy 2012). Can God lie? He speaks to us only indirectly.

God followed, rather, a norm suited to his nature as supreme creator: "Use your supreme wisdom and love in designing the world." And so God designed the world to make life not easy or pleasant, but rather intensely meaningful. God put us on a challenging journey toward eternal life, where we struggle against evil to grow in wisdom and love. Our final destiny will be more valuable and meaningful because it comes after a long struggle.

Rational norms: God, as a rational being, is subject to RAT: "In making important decisions, be vividly aware of the facts, avoid falsehoods, and be consistent." As a perfect being, he'd seemingly satisfy this perfectly. But would he really satisfy golden-rule consistency? Is God, in creating the world, treating suffering humans as he's willing that he'd be treated in their place? Some doubt this, thinking that the world's pain and suffering is too much; the pain isn't worth the gain. And so God, they think, would fail the GR test: he wouldn't be willing that he himself (or someone he loves dearly) be subjected to so much pain and suffering for the sake of an heroically meaningful life.

Believers contend that the gain *is* worth the pain from the view of eternity, and that God *does* satisfy GR. Christianity makes a strong point here: God sent his Son to struggle against physical pain and mental suffering on the cross, to express his supreme love for humanity in a powerful way. So God *was* willing that he himself (or someone he loves dearly) endure severe pain and suffering for the sake of supremely meaningful love. So God satisfies GR as he treats us in a loving but Irenaean way. That's part of the message of the cross and resurrection.

8.3 Further Issues

(Q1) Does God have duties?

We naturally speak of God "doing right and good," but it's odd to speak of God "doing his duty" or "doing what he ought to do." These sound odd, perhaps, because "ought" and "duty" suggest that the action is a burden that goes against contrary inclinations, which wouldn't apply to God.

In place of "ought" and "duty," we can speak of God "doing the right action." When we say "A is the right action," this means that A is right (permissible) and omitting A is wrong (not permissible). This is close to "ought" and "duty," but doesn't carry suggestions about contrary inclinations.

(Q2) What do we mean when we call God "good"?

We can mean three things (or even all three at once).

(1) God does only actions that are right and good, and never what is wrong and bad. This follows from general facts about God's nature – that he knows everything and is consistent. Since God knows everything, he knows all moral truths; and since he's consistent, his actions accord with these.

(2) God is wise and loving, and has further virtues (like being just and merciful). This too rests on general facts about God's nature. And God calls us to eternal life with him.

(3) God gives each of us special gifts. Since all we have is from God, we can see God's goodness in our talents, our health, or the beauty of a canyon. We can't say that God wouldn't have been good if he hadn't given us these gifts; he might instead have given us a challenge, perhaps sickness instead of health. God gives us such things at his discretion; he can quite rightly make different choices about them. Even challenges that God sends us, like sicknesses, are intended for our good; they too can be "special gifts" for us *if we respond properly*. Ignatius of Loyola (1524) suggested that we pray to be *indifferent* about whether God ultimately sends us gifts or challenges (like health or sickness), desiring only what helps us serve God better;[5] this is a wise but very challenging attitude for believers to have about personal evils.

---

[5] One of God's "special gifts" for Ignatius was a cannonball that shattered his leg; his recovery changed his life. Challenges can promote growth.

(Q3) Is each evil required for a greater good (so the total good wouldn't be as great if the evil hadn't occurred)?

No. If each evil is required for a greater good, then why fight evil (since then the evil we fight is required for a greater good)? And why not cause evil ourselves (since then this evil will bring about a greater good)? If each evil is required for a greater good, then it doesn't matter whether we fight evil or cause evil.

It's important that our actions can make a difference, that the world can be genuinely better or worse depending on how we act. Only then can our actions be significant.

My answer assumes that it makes at least rough sense to speak of the "total" good. Some see different kinds of value as incommensurable; so we can't add up moral good and physical evil to get a "total." This would make question Q3 meaningless.

(Q4) Why doesn't God let us freely choose what to do and then block the bad consequences of our wrong actions?

If God did this, then again our actions wouldn't be significant. Consider that we can love our children or beat them. If we beat them, then they'll suffer; God normally won't step in to block this. How we act is significant because it can make a big difference to people's lives. Having God block our action's bad consequences would rob our action of significance.

(Q5) Does God want us to be happy? If he does, and if he can make us happy, then why are most people so miserable? (Hume 1779: Part 10)

Pleasure differs from happiness. *Pleasure* is an enjoyable feeling; *happiness* is an overall contentment with our life based on understanding how our life connects with wider purposes. We might have many pleasures but be unhappy, seeing our life of pleasures as ultimately meaningless. Or we might have few pleasures but be happy, seeing our life as deeply meaningful, as making a difference to people's lives. God wants us to be happy but cares little about whether we have a life of pleasure.

Why are so many people miserable? Mainly they look for happiness in wrong place, in self-interest and immediate pleasure. The real tragedy in life isn't to suffer pain, but rather to live in a way that's selfish and without meaning.[6]

Why doesn't God *make* us happy? The key to happiness is to live properly, as God intended: *to care about others in a meaningful life.* In other words, we need *love and faith*; this gains us a hundredfold here and eternal life hereafter (§7.2). But we can choose otherwise, since God made us free.

(Q6) Why didn't God create us morally perfect already? Why does God make it so difficult to do the right thing?

Virtue formed after a difficult struggle is more valuable and meaningful (§6.5.6) than virtue that we're just given. As Irenaeus put it long ago, "And the harder we strive, so much is it the more valuable. And indeed those things are not esteemed so highly which come spontaneously, as those which are reached by much anxious care" (Swindal 2005: 55).

(Q7) Why do the good often suffer while the evil prosper?

Suppose that the good always prospered while the evil suffered. Then it would become clear that doing the right thing always promotes self-interest. This would make impossible the struggle between doing the right thing and doing what *seems* to promote self-interest; and that would be a great loss, since such struggles are very significant. So, even though right actions may always serve our self-interest (taking into account the afterlife), this shouldn't be too obvious in our present life.

(Q8) Why did God make my mother suffer so much from rheumatoid arthritis? Did God want her to suffer?

God didn't cause or desire this specific evil. But this evil accords with a structure that God set up; a certain percentage of people will get such diseases. We can understand in general terms why God set up this structure. These evils are given to us so that we can grow by responding in love. God gives us the ability to make such evils be an occasion of love and growth (as it mostly was for my mother and family). If we instead respond with bitterness, that's our fault; God at least gave us the *option* to give a loving response that has great value.

---

[6] External circumstances have less to do with overall happiness than most people think. A famous study (Brickman 1978) compared million-dollar lottery winners with quadriplegic accident victims; a year later there wasn't much difference in their happiness levels. Other research shows that the blind, retarded, and malformed aren't less happy than other people.

I had two students in class, let's call them Mike and Ann, who met in freshman biology and grew ever closer. After graduation, Mike got a rare cancer and almost died; this brought them even closer together. When I did their wedding ceremony, the key words, which both parties repeat, stood out: "I promise to be true to you in good times and in bad, *in sickness and in health*; I will love you and honor you all the days of my life." Mike and Ann had a beautiful love for each other, a love deepened by sickness and suffering. My homily mentioned Irenaeus, which they read in my class: "He wrote about the role of evil and suffering in a world created by a loving God; he saw life as a difficult but meaningful struggle against evil, by which we grow into greater faith and love." And so it was for Mike and Ann.

Our suffering is a gift from God that can deepen our lives. How we respond is up to us; if we reject it and become bitter, that's our fault, not God's. Mike and Ann could have responded to cancer with bitterness and despair (which would have been out of character). We're here, ultimately, to care for each other – in sickness and in health, in good times and in bad – with a love that mirrors God's love for us. God calls us to a life that can be difficult and painful, but also deeply meaningful.

(Q9) Augustine (400) said that our lives are so jumbled and random that it's difficult to discern a divine plan behind them. But God's care for us is clear from *reason* (how well God designed our bodies) and *revelation* (how Christ lived, died, and rose for us). So it's better to see God as having a plan for us that's inscrutable. Do you agree?

Not entirely. We can grasp at least part of God's plan. God intends that *we struggle to grow in wisdom and love through difficult and chaotic situations*. Our lives have ups and downs, setbacks and tragedies, and crazy events that confuse and challenge and push us to grow. That's what God intended. And so the messiness of our lives *is* part of God's plan.

(Q10) When God punishes sinners to eternal damnation, is this compatible with God being supremely loving?

I believe in heaven and hell and in punishment for wrongdoing. But I don't think that *God* punishes us; instead, we punish ourselves. If we separate ourselves from God, temporarily or forever, we keep ourselves from our supreme fulfillment and happiness. We're made for God, and without God, we'll be miserable. The worst way to punish ourselves is to reject God permanently, forever; this would be eternal damnation. But while free creatures *could* choose this, does it ever happen? Maybe God keeps giving people a second (and third, and...) chance to change, and so all are saved eventually. Or maybe God destroys one who'd never convert, to prevent endless suffering. A good God would likely do such things; so I doubt that anyone actually suffers *eternal* damnation (see Hick 1979: 337–52).

(Q11) What does Irenaean theodicy commit us to?

It commits us to reject hedonism, to accept free will, and to accept that virtue reached after a struggle can have more value. And it leads to beliefs about God's purposes in creating us.

(Q12) Given that God's plan requires *some* suffering, doesn't the world have *excessive* suffering?

John Hick (1978: 327–36) thinks "excessive" is relative, so we can object the same way in a world with less suffering. If the most horrible suffering was eliminated, lesser suffering would become the "most horrible" – and we could similarly argue that God should eliminate it. Eventually there would be no suffering – which would frustrate God's goals. So Hick has doubts about the "excessive suffering" objection. But he's not entirely happy with this answer and later talks about the *mystery of evil*.

Irenaean theodicy may have further problems. Its goal isn't to fulfill the impossible task of giving a complete account of evil in God's plan; there'll always be mystery in evil and in everything else we seek to understand (like the weather). Instead, we need to account for evil well enough to defend against atheistic arguments from evil. I think we *can* achieve this limited goal.

(Q13) Irenaean theodicy is plausible and consistent, but is there evidence that it's true? Why think that there's a God at all, and one that works in an Irenaean manner?

Irenaean theodicy is a *defensive strategy* (Hick 1978). We don't prove it; instead, we give it as a plausible possibility to counter atheistic arguments. We can defend it as plausible in terms of logic, science, morality, and our religious tradition.

(Q14) There's also a scriptural problem of evil.[7] The sacred texts of Christianity and other religions seem at times to teach cruelty, like the killing of innocent women and children. Psalm 137:9 prays about enemies: "Blessed is the one who takes their infants and smashes them against the rocks." Is this God's teaching?

If you search the Web for *evil old testament God*, you'll find that believers try to answer in two ways. Some defend the killing, saying that the enemies were warned beforehand and were so corrupt that their innocent children would someday become very evil. Others condemn such killing and take the approach that I sketch here (adapted from Copan 2008, 2011). This second approach assumes, with most educated believers, that God didn't dictate the Bible word for word; instead, God moved humans to express his message in their own human way.

Ancient peoples often used exaggerated language that shouldn't be taken literally. The Bible sometimes says that the Israelites *did kill all the Canaanites* – men, women, children, and animals; but years later, they're still fighting Canaanites, so evidently the language was exaggerated. The New Testament also uses exaggerated language. So it says that we cannot enter the Kingdom of God unless we *hate* our father and mother. It really means that we cannot enter the Kingdom if we love our father and mother more than we love God.

We sometimes use such exaggerated language today. When I studied at Michigan, I sang a parody of our rival's fight song: "*Annihilate* Ohio State, and humble Woody Hayes!" I never literally wanted *annihilation*: to totally destroy and obliterate them, perhaps by nuclear bombs. No, all I wanted was to beat their football team. Sometimes we (and the biblical writers) use overly macho language that shouldn't be taken literally.

Ancient Israelites were often morally crude. Even King David did very evil things; these aren't necessarily approved. While biblical rules were often by today's standards crude, they were by ancient Near Eastern standards innovative and egalitarian, motivated by the biblical insight that we're all created in the "image and likeness of God" (Genesis 1:27). Old Testament rules weren't meant to hold forever; they were intended rather

---

[7] Dawkins (2006: 31) wrote, "The God of the Old Testament is arguably the most unpleasant character in all of fiction: jealous and proud of it; a petty, unjust, unforgiving control-freak; a vindictive, bloodthirsty ethnic cleanser; a misogynistic, homophobic, racist, infanticidal, genocidal, filicidal, pestilential, megalomaniacal, sadomasochistic, capriciously malevolent bully."

to lift a crude and barbaric people a little higher. So Jesus in Matthew 19:8 said that Moses approved of divorce because of the "hardness of the hearts" of the people, who weren't then ready for a higher law; Paul in Galatians 3:24 called the Jewish law "a tutor" to help Israel prepare the way for Christ. God sometimes works gradually, trying to lift us to a higher standard little by little.

Copan often appeals to other factors, like the meaning of words, different ways to translate or interpret a passage, and cultural background information. It's dangerous to pick random statements written thousands of years ago and, in ignorance of linguistic and historical context, draw big conclusions. Many who appeal to the scriptural problem of evil do just that.

A common approach to interpreting the Bible that goes back to St. Augustine emphasizes that the Bible *centrally* teaches that God is loving and that we're to love our neighbor as ourselves. Whatever *seems* to go against this must be interpreted as not literal. So we have to look at language ambiguities, cultural context, and so forth.[8]

An Iranian philosophy grad student at the University of Tehran, Mohammed Karimi, e-mailed me about a similar problem in Islam. Muslim scriptures, like Christian ones, have passages that convey a golden-rule or love-your-neighbor view, as well as ones that seem cruel and divisive; which should we follow? This is a practical problem in many religious countries. I answered much like the above, and emphasized that we should interpret difficult passages in terms of the religion's central teachings, which would be GR and love your neighbor.[9]

I got an e-mail from someone objecting to my claim that all the great world religions endorse GR. He said Islam didn't endorse GR, and he mentioned Koran 48:29 about being "ruthless to unbelievers but merciful to one another." I suggested that he do a Web search to see how Muslim scholars take the passage (most translations are softer than "ruthless," using words like "forceful" and "firm of heart"). I added that Christianity too has verses that seem to violate GR, and that we need to see how Christian scholars take these verses before drawing conclusions. Again,

[8] Major Christian thinkers of early centuries, including Origen and Augustine, thought we need serious study to see what to take literally and what to take figuratively. See Swindal (2005: 75–76, 101).

[9] http://www.acommonword.com has a strong statement that's massively supported across Islam on the centrality of love of God and neighbor (the latter expressed as GR). Karimi claims (and I'd agree) that GR, being rational and global, has priority as we interpret difficult passages; God created us all with the capacity to know GR.

we need to treat another's faith by the same standards that we want our own faith to be treated (§6.6).

(Q15) Isn't the God story too convenient to be true? "A loving God created us in his image and likeness, and destined us to an eternal life that fulfills all our hopes and dreams." Maybe we made up this story ourselves.

Or maybe God made us to find our fulfillment in him – and this is why the God story fits our hopes and dreams. But is there any evidence for God?

8.4 Evidence for God

We now move to the *unnecessary hypothesis* objection. I propose this formulation:

> We ought to posit God's existence if and only if God is part of our best explanation of the empirical world.
> God isn't part of our best explanation of the empirical world. (Our best explanation is *science*, which doesn't need God.)
> ∴ We ought not to posit God's existence.

The atheist Dawkins (1995: 132–33) claimed that the observable universe shows no signs of design or purpose: "The universe we observe has precisely the properties we should expect if there is, at bottom, no design, no purpose, no evil and no good, nothing but blind pitiless indifference." I'll later dispute this and I'll argue (against premise 2) that God *is* part of our best explanation of the empirical world.

I also have doubts about premise 1. Its generalized form ("We ought to accept A if and only if A is part of our best explanation of the empirical world") would outlaw logical rules, scientific-method norms, and itself – since none of these is part of our best explanation of the empirical world.

Belief in God has been defended on many grounds: religious instincts or feelings, mystical experience, our need for meaning, pragmatic life consequences, a priori arguments, and so on. I don't want to reject all these: *God gives us many paths to belief* (and we don't all get the same path). For many, religious beliefs are naturally attractive and philosophy is needed only to answer objections. To deal with scientifically minded skeptics, however, it's useful to give reasoning that uses scientific data.

I sometimes ask my classes this question (Gensler 2011b):

If you were God, how much evidence would you give for your existence? Would you give (a) conclusive evidence, (b) strong evidence, (c) weak evidence, or (d) no evidence?

I have students think about the choices and then vote for one. I tell them that, since they're just expressing their mind, there's no right or wrong answer beyond that. I add that I'd be disappointed if some options don't get any votes.

Conclusive evidence option (a) gets about 10 percent of the vote. Supporters say, "To live their lives, humans need to know clearly that I exist; so I'd give indisputable evidence and proof about this." Some say they'd use a loud voice from heaven! Those who pick (a) are often skeptical about God's existence.[10]

Strong evidence (b) gets 40 percent of the vote. Supporters say, "While it's important for us to have some strong indication that there's a God, it's also important for us to struggle with this issue – so our belief is to some extent our personal choice. So I wouldn't provide an indisputable proof of my existence."

Weak evidence (c) also gets 40 percent of the vote. Supporters say, "While it's important for us to have *some* sign that there's a God, this needs to be weak and ambiguous, so our belief is mostly from personal struggle and choice."

No evidence (d) gets only 10 percent of the vote. Supporters say, "We need to struggle and form our own belief about God; it's less important that we get the right answer."

I think there's *strong evidence* (b) for God's existence, based in part on recent science. This new evidence is stronger than the traditional proofs, which I think give only *weak evidence* (c).

8.5 In the Beginning

The Bible starts boldly (Genesis 1:1): "*In the beginning, God created the heavens and the earth.*" Atheists reject God but could go either way about a beginning. The traditional atheist view I call *classical atheism*: there's

---

[10] Some atheists argue from *hiddenness*: "If there's a God, then he'd provide conclusive evidence for his existence. But there's no such evidence. Therefore, there's no God." Most of my students think God *wouldn't* give us conclusive evidence. Hick (1978: 281–82) argues that moral freedom requires that God's existence not be too clear to us; see also Moser (2008).

no God, and the world had no beginning (it always was and always will be). While believers thought the world needed a cause, atheists thought a *world* with no beginning or cause was just as plausible as a *God* with no beginning or cause. Many saw this issue as a stalemate, since science couldn't decide it either way (§2.2).

Science later attacked classical atheism. It turns out that the world isn't eternal but began to exist 13.75 billion years ago in a big bang explosion.[11] The Doppler effect and the redshift provide evidence. The *Doppler effect* is the change in sound (or light) waves from an object that's coming toward you or going away. Imagine that a race car comes toward you, passes you, and then goes away; the car sound goes from a higher pitch to a lower pitch as the car passes you:

- Car sounds coming toward you have a higher pitch, more beats per second: //////////.
- Car sounds going away from you have a lower pitch, fewer beats per second: / / / / / /.

Hum a high pitch as the car comes toward you, then a low pitch as it goes away. Motion toward you compresses sound waves (more beats per second, higher pitch) while motion away expands them (fewer beats per second, lower pitch). *Colors* work the same way. A yellow car would look slightly green coming toward you and slightly orange going away; but this shift would be too small to observe unless the car were going extremely fast.

The *redshift* is the observed fact that colors from distant stars get shifted toward red. So a heated element that's known to be yellow becomes slightly orange. Scientists explain this by the Doppler effect and the movement of distant stars away from us (the expanding universe). Winding back the process, we can compute when the world exploded from an initial point, in the big bang. Scientists are getting better at dating this event; the current figure is between 13.6 and 13.9 billion years.

A longer story would discuss background radiation (which strengthens the argument), entropy (the world would have reached almost complete entropy had it existed forever), and much math. We won't go into details. The multiple-big-bang theory, which says that the world goes through an infinite cycle of expansions and contractions, used to be popular. Fewer hold this today, since calculations seem to show that the density of matter

---

[11] Georges Lemaître, a Catholic priest, first proposed this in the 1930s; he spoke of "the Cosmic Egg exploding at the moment of creation."

in the world isn't enough to bring about contraction through gravity.[12] So our best science supports the view that the world is a one-shot process and had a beginning in time.

But if the world began to exist long ago, then surely something had to cause its beginning – and what else could this be but a great mind? The kalam argument (named for a medieval Islamic argument) begins this way:

> Whatever began to exist had a cause.
> The world began to exist.
> ∴ The world had a cause.

Premise 1 is based on commonsense metaphysics and applies only to beings that *begin to exist*; so it says nothing about whether an *eternal* God or world needs a cause. Premise 2 is based on current physics (and perhaps also on arguments about the impossibility of an actual physical infinite). Given "The world had a cause," we can continue:

> The world had a cause.
> Every cause is either material (based on antecedent conditions and causal
>   laws) or personal (based on free will).
> ∴ The world had a material or a personal cause.

Premise 2 is commonsense metaphysics (based on our inability to conceive of any third kind of cause). Finally, we argue:

> The world had a material or a personal cause.
> The world didn't have a material cause.
> ∴ The world had a personal cause (God).

Premise 2 is true because *the world* by definition contains all matter, and nothing can cause itself. The conclusion follows (taking "God" in the minimal sense of "the personal cause of the world"). So Genesis 1:1 ("In the beginning, God created the heavens and the earth") can be based on reason *and* faith.[13]

I take this to be a fairly strong argument. What does J. L. Mackie, my favorite atheist philosopher, say about it? He's convinced from the problem of evil that there's no God. So he raises doubts about two premises (1982: 45–49). Against "Whatever began to exist had a cause," maybe the world just popped into existence without a cause. (I see this

---

[12] Hawking (1998: 45–49). He also argues that an eternal, nonexpanding world is unstable: gravity over an infinite time would eventually collapse it.

[13] For more on kalam, see Craig (1994: 91–125) and Spitzer (2010: 13–103). Kalam combines science (one premise) with metaphysics (three premises).

as weird and implausible, like the student excuse "An uncaused elephant popped into existence and ate my homework," but not entirely refutable.) Or against "The world began to exist," maybe current science is wrong and the world is eternal. (This is possible too, but the evidence is stronger now than when Mackie wrote; and this move makes atheism look bad, since it rejects our best current science on religious grounds.)

Many atheists, accepting that the world is 14 billion years old, moved from *classical atheism* to *big bang atheism*:

- *Classical atheism*: There's no God, and the world had no beginning in time.
- *Big bang atheism*: There's no God, but the world had a beginning in time.

Big bang atheism is less plausible. Before recent advances in physics, few if any atheists thought that the world had a beginning. I pity atheists who now have to explain to their children, "We atheists believe the world just popped into existence, without any cause, 14 billion years ago!" This may move atheist children to question their atheism.

But wait, it only gets worse for atheists.

8.6 Fine-Tuning

Before Darwin, atheists had trouble explaining how humans could have appeared without God. The only other option was that we resulted from a random mixing of chemicals – you shake chemicals together randomly and end up with a pair of humans; but this is very implausible.

Darwin gave a better option: humans, and other species, came to be in an evolutionary process by *mutation* and *selection*. *Mutation* means that a species randomly produces organisms with slight differences; so some are bigger or faster. *Selection* means that those with some features are more likely to survive and produce offspring with these same features. Having millions of mutation-selection cycles produces radically new life-forms, including humans. Thomas Huxley (1866: 297) saw the implications for nonbelievers:

[Darwin freed] us forever from the dilemma – Refuse to accept the creation hypothesis, and what have you to propose that can be accepted by any cautious reasoner? In 1857 I had no answer.... My reflection [later]... was, "How extremely stupid not to have thought of that!"

So Darwin seemingly lets us explain, without mentioning God, how humans came to be.[14]

Here's a longer explanation (Lewis 1952: 21–22). The universe has lots of stars. Let's suppose there's a one in a thousand chance that a star will *produce planets with liquid water*.[15] And let's suppose there's a one in a thousand chance that a planet with liquid water will *produce life*. And let's suppose there's a one in a thousand chance that a planet with life will *produce intelligent life*. Then, for a given star, there's a one in a billion (1,000 × 1,000 × 1,000) chance that it'll produce intelligent life. A Web search suggests that there are approximately 70,000,000,000,000,000,000,000,000 (7×10^{22}) stars. If intelligent life evolved in a billionth of these, then 70,000,000,000,000 (7×10^{13}) planets would have intelligent life. Even if these numbers are far off, still a huge random universe can easily evolve intelligent life.

Or maybe not. Brandon Carter (1973) studied what physics is needed for thinking life to exist. It turns out that the physical laws and constants have to be within an extremely narrow range to make such life possible. Steven Hawking (Carter's physics colleague at Cambridge) gave this example (1998: 126): "If the rate of expansion one second after the big bang had been smaller by even one part in a hundred thousand million million, the world would have recollapsed before it ever reached its present size." This would have prevented life. So the value has to be correct to the seventeenth decimal place for life to evolve. Hawking (1998: 129–30) goes on (my italics):

The laws of science, as we know them at present, contain many fundamental numbers, like the size of the electric charge of the electron and the ratio of the masses of the proton and the electron.... *The values of these numbers seem to have been very finely adjusted to make possible the development of life.* For example, if the electric charge of the electron had been only slightly different, stars either would have been unable to burn hydrogen and helium, or else they would not have exploded.... There are relatively few ranges of values for the numbers that would allow the development of any form of intelligent life....[16] *One can take this either as evidence of a divine purpose in Creation*

---

[14] I'll ignore another huge issue: how do random processes produce living organisms with a complex genetic structure, as needed by evolution?

[15] Such planets are said to be in the *Goldilocks zone*, after the fable character who liked her porridge not too hot and not too cold.

[16] Many universes have no stars or no heavy elements. Few could produce life, even with a wide understanding of what's needed for life (on which life needn't require water and needn't be carbon based).

and the choice of the laws of science or as support for the strong anthropic principle.[17]

Could the world by pure chance be so finely tuned that it can produce life? This seem very improbable. It's more likely that the world was created by an intelligent being (God) who designed it very carefully to bring forth life.

I created a Windows computer game to illustrate fine-tuning. Go to http://www.harryhiker.com, click <u>Software</u> at the top, and then click <u>Genesis</u>. A message pops up: "The object of this game is to set up the basic laws of your universe so that life will eventually evolve. If your universe brings forth life, you win; otherwise, you lose." Then the program appears:

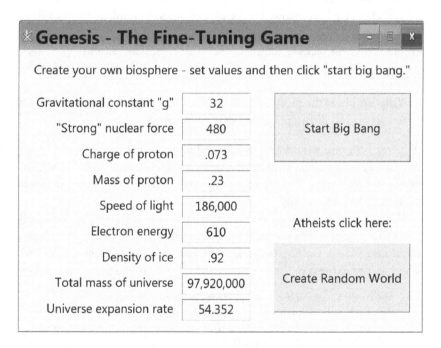

Genesis - The Fine-Tuning Game

Create your own biosphere - set values and then click "start big bang."

Gravitational constant "g"	32	
"Strong" nuclear force	480	**Start Big Bang**
Charge of proton	.073	
Mass of proton	.23	
Speed of light	186,000	
Electron energy	610	Atheists click here:
Density of ice	.92	
Total mass of universe	97,920,000	**Create Random World**
Universe expansion rate	54.352	

You set values for the constants and then click *Start Big Bang*. You'll get a noise and a message: "Sorry, but your world self-destructed and didn't produce life. Please try again." Under "Atheists click here," there's a

---

[17] "Strong anthropic principle" is what I call *parallel worlds* (but others call *multiverse*); Hawking criticizes this idea. For more on the fine-tuning argument, see F. Collins (2006: 63–84), R. Collins (1999), Flew (2007: 85–158), Glynn (1997: 21–55), Manson (2003), Plantinga (2011: 193–224), Spitzer (2010: 13–103), and Swinburne (2004: 172–88).

Create Random World button. This puts random numbers into the constants and then creates a world. You'll again get a noise and a message: "Sorry, but your world self-destructed and didn't produce life. The RANDOM button gives you a chance to produce life of one in 100 trillion." Students like the program, which nicely explains fine-tuning.

My program, however, has limitations:

- It needs more decimal places. The expansion rate has to be correct to the *seventeenth decimal place* for life to evolve.
- It lacks units. Should you give the speed of light in *miles per hour* or *kilometers per second*?
- It needs more physical constants (I give only nine). I don't know how many there are.[18]
- The chance of producing life by giving random numbers to the values is *much less* than 1 in 100 trillion.
- The program lacks a parallel-worlds option. This would open multiple copies of the program using randomly different values for the constants.
- You can't beat the program and produce life. I didn't know the correct values and so didn't put them into my program.

A better program would give words and animations for the world based on your values: maybe your world lacks stars, collapses quickly, or contains only hydrogen. But my program, even as it is, nicely helps students to understand fine-tuning.

We need to express the fine-tuning argument more carefully. Let's call a world *fine-tuned* if its physical laws and constants (like the gravitational constant g) are in the narrow range of what's required for intelligent life. Then we can express the argument as an *inference to the best explanation*:

> We ought to accept the best explanation for fine-tuning.
> The best explanation for fine-tuning is that an intelligent being intending to create intelligent life created the world (this is a better explanation than *chance* or *parallel worlds*).
> ∴ We ought to accept that an intelligent being (God) intending to create intelligent life created the world.[19]

---

[18] http://www.godandscience.org/apologetics/designun.html gives thirty-four constants and tells about what happens to your universe if these are a little too high or too low. http://www.godandscience.org/apologetics/quotes.html has quotes from many scientists about the universe's design.

[19] Note carefully the premises and conclusion. People sometimes distort the reasoning (e.g., "The fine-tuning argument claims that an unlikely event can't happen – or, if it does, then we must bring in God to explain it").

Premise 1 rests on the idea that the world is fine-tuned, which in general is solid even though there are controversies about details. The big dispute is how this fact of fine-tuning is to be explained, and whether it even needs an explanation.

The *chance explanation* says that it just happened that the world was finely tuned for life. Sure, it was a long shot; but long shots sometimes pay off – hey, people *do* win the lottery. This gives a third atheist alternative to Genesis 1:1:

Big-gamble big bang atheism: There's no God, the world 14 billion years ago popped into existence without a cause, and the basic physical laws and constants just happened (in a zillion-to-one coincidence) to be in the narrow range that makes life possible.

But this seems extraordinarily implausible.

Another explanation mentions "parallel worlds," which are complete and real universes entirely separate from each other, so there's no causal interaction or travel between them. This explanation posits an infinity of parallel worlds, each governed by a different physics; it's highly likely that *some* of these would produce life. There can be no evidence for parallel worlds; but they do permit an atheist worldview that makes the emergence of intelligent life probable. This gives us a fourth atheist alternative to Genesis 1:1:

Parallel-worlds big bang atheism: There's no God. But there are an infinity of parallel worlds. Each popped into existence without a cause, and each runs by a different set of basic physical laws and constants. Our world happens to be one of the few that produced life.

This Ockham's-razor nightmare seems extraordinarily implausible. Genesis 1:1 ("In the beginning, God created the heavens and the earth") is far simpler and more intuitive.

I have my students vote on which explanation they'd prefer if they were atheists: *big gamble* or *parallel worlds*. While they have a hard time taking either seriously, science-fiction fans often pick parallel worlds.

I take fine-tuning to be a strong argument. The simplest and best explanation for fine-tuning involves God: the world was caused by a great mind who "fine-tuned" its physical laws to make possible the evolution of intelligent life.

Francis Collins (2006), a prominent atheistic scientist who led the Human Genome Project that mapped human genes, accepted the fine-tuning argument, came to believe in God, and became a strong Christian; accepting God changed his life. Antony Flew (2007), a prominent atheistic philosopher who spent much of his life attacking theism, also accepted the argument and came to believe in God – but a deistic God, not one who reveals himself; believing in God had less effect on his wider life (although it did shake up his philosophy).

J. L. Mackie (1982: 141) made two remarks about the argument:

- He says we have no idea what worlds would result from other physical constants, and so we can't say that they couldn't have produced life. But scientists think we *do* know much about this. Hawking mentions constant values that yield lifeless worlds that immediately collapse, lack stars, have only light elements like hydrogen, or whatever.
- Some debunk fine-tuning by saying, "Of course the physical laws and constants are just right to allow us to have evolved. We shouldn't find this surprising, since otherwise we wouldn't be here." Mackie thinks this is a poor objection, since we *can* consider alternative possibilities (which do not include our being there to experience them).

Sober (2009: 77) uses this second objection; he argues (against premise 1) that fine-tuning needs no explanation:

The standard criticism of this argument invokes some version of the *anthropic principle*. The rough idea is that, since we are alive, we are bound to observe that the constants are right, regardless of whether the values of those constants were caused by ID [Intelligent Design] or by Chance. We are the victims of an *observational selection effect.*[20]

So of course observers can conclude, since they're alive, that the laws of physics are consistent with their being alive. Thus fine-tuning (that the laws of physics happen to be consistent with the existence of human life) can be expected, is unremarkable, and needs no explanation.

This objection rests on a confusion. If observers are bound to observe some fact, that doesn't show that this fact requires no explanation. Here are examples:

- You're reading this sentence. This shows *that* you know English. But it doesn't explain *why* you know English. The explanation might be that you learned English as you grew up in an English-speaking country.
- You hurt your neck in a car accident. This shows *that* there was a car accident but not *why* it happened. The explanation might be that

---

[20] Sober's "ID" is misleading, because "intelligent design" usually refers to an antievolution *creationism* – which differs greatly from *fine-tuning*.

another driver was sending a text message, lost control, and went into your lane.

- The concert pianist gushes about how good your piano sounds. This shows *that* it's finely tuned but not *why* it's finely tuned. The explanation might be that you recently hired someone to tune it.
- You exist. This shows *that* the laws of physics happen to be consistent with the existence of human life. But it doesn't explain *why* the laws of physics happen to be consistent with the existence of human life. The explanation might be chance, parallel worlds, or design.

This approach suggests a fifth atheist alternative to Genesis 1:1:

Observation-selection big bang atheism: There's no God, the world 14 billion years ago popped into existence without a cause, and the basic physical laws and constants just happened (in a zillion-to-one coincidence) to be in the narrow range which would make life possible. But, since our existence shows *that* the laws of physics happen to be consistent with the existence of human life, we needn't worry about *why* the laws of physics happen to be consistent with the existence of human life.

This is as crazy as the *big gamble* and *parallel worlds* options. The further we investigate, the more Genesis 1:1 looks much more plausible than any of its alternatives.

One of my students had another objection. He conceded that fine-tuning was a fact and that the nontheistic explanations for it were poor. But he thought the Great Mind idea was poor too, since it clashes with how we think about the world; so it has a very small antecedent probability (see also Dawkins 2006: Chapter 3). Thus we have no idea how to explain fine-tuning.

My response had three parts. (1) The Great Mind idea *does* explain the constants in a familiar and straightforward way; we've all experienced minds working out complex details to get a given result (e.g., working out a house plan in order to have a fine, livable home). (2) The Great Mind idea accords with how most people explain the origin of the universe, as resulting from a divine plan; here, too, it beats the alternatives. (3) The Great Mind idea may seem less likely to someone who thinks, for example, that *only matter exists*. But why think this? And isn't such thinking flawed if it makes us conclude that there's no good explanation of the universe as we know it?

The kalam and fine-tuning arguments seem strong. But there are reasons for not seeing them as conclusive:

- While these arguments are based on our best current science, science could change and go in another direction.
- While alternatives to these arguments (like parallel worlds or worlds popping into existence without a cause) seem flimsy, we can't show that they're impossible.
- Many intelligent people reject these arguments. While their objections seem weak, maybe we're missing something – or maybe stronger objections will appear later.
- The fine-tuning argument uses an *inductive* inference to the best explanation, which isn't as clear-cut as *deduction*.[21]

So kalam and fine-tuning, while strong, don't *force* belief on us. There's still room for struggle and personal choice.

8.7 Concluding Issues

(Q1) How does science connect to the big philosophical questions about ethics and religion?

Science can't by itself answer such questions; it can't by itself show how we ought to live, whether there are objective moral truths, or whether there's a God. At times, science may *seem* to answer such questions by itself; but carefully working out the *reasoning* will reveal essential unstated nonscientific premises. Kalam and fine-tuning, for example, appeal to scientific data; but deriving conclusions about God requires adding metaphysical premises (for kalam) or normative premises about what explanations to accept or prefer (for fine-tuning).

Atheistic popular science often gives scientific data and then draws a "scientific conclusion" about there being no objective moral truths or no God. We need to ask, What further premises are needed to draw the conclusion by strict logical standards? And are these further premises defensible?

Science, however, isn't entirely *neutral* on the big questions about ethics and religion. We philosophers argue about philosophical questions using whatever data we can find, including scientific findings. It's much easier to defend the golden rule as a central moral truth, for example, if

---

[21] See Gensler (2010: 112–17). We can raise questions like these: on what grounds is one explanation *better* than another? Should we accept the *best possible* explanation (even though no one has thought of it) or the *best available* explanation (even though all current explanations are poor)? And why is the best explanation most likely to be the true one?

our best science shows (as it does) that GR is practically universal across the different cultures of the world, rather than if it showed (as it doesn't) that GR is psychologically impossible to follow. And it's much easier to defend belief in God on recent physics (which includes fine-tuning and the big bang) than on older physics.

So I take a middle position. I deny that science by itself can prove religious (or antireligious) conclusions; I also deny that science and religion are entirely separate (as Gould 1997 suggests). Instead, I contend that both areas connect somewhat and that we may be able to defend or attack religious views from scientific views if we add further philosophical premises.

Recent science is friendlier to God. Besides big bang and fine-tuning, much else has changed over the last fifty years. Freud's negative views about religion have been extensively criticized; empirically, religion isn't a harmful neurosis but instead greatly benefits health and happiness. Studies of near-death experiences suggest that the afterlife is real. And mainstream philosophy too is friendlier to theism, due to logical positivism's demise, Plantinga's work and example, and Christian philosophy's rising importance. Atheistic arguments are often based on very outdated views.[22]

(Q2) Do kalam and fine-tuning show the inadequacy of some atheistic claims considered earlier?

Yes, here are examples:

(1) *"Religion lacks evidence and is discredited by science."* Kalam and fine-tuning show otherwise.

(2) *"The huge size of the universe and the random factors that produced humans show that humans have no special place (no privileged position) in this purposeless world."* Fine-tuning shows otherwise: the basic structure of the world (scientific laws and constants) was set up in order to produce intelligent life. And so intelligent beings (including us and maybe others on far-off planets) are of central importance to the universe.

(3) *"Feeling pulls us toward religion, while reason pulls us away; we should follow reason instead of feeling."* With kalam and fine-tuning, reason and feeling pull together, toward belief in God. Faith needn't fear reason, if reason is pursued deeply.

---

[22] See Glynn (1997), Moser and Copan (2003: 1–2), Plantinga (2011), and Smith (2001).

(4) "*Our best explanation of the world is science, which doesn't need God.*" But we need God to explain how the world came to be 14 billion years ago, and why the world is regulated by a very improbable combination of physical constants that makes intelligent life possible. So it's more reasonable to say (§7.2.2) that "evolution brought about humans, and God brought about evolution in order to bring about humans."

(Q3) What are the wider ethical and religious implications of kalam and fine-tuning?

Kalam and fine-tuning make these claims:

K. The world began to exist and had a personal cause (God).
F. The world was created by an intelligent being (God), who wanted to produce intelligent life and who set up the world with great precision in order to bring about this result.

Kalam (K) supports God's existence (which is central to theistic religion and theistic ethics) and is much like Genesis 1:1 ("*In the beginning, God created the heavens and the earth*"). So we have reason backing up faith on a basic issue; St. Thomas Aquinas would be pleased.

Fine-tuning (F) goes further, talking about *God as an intelligent being* who acts with the intention of *bringing about intelligent creatures*. In biblical terms, God created us in his "image and likeness" (Genesis 1:27). Of course, humans (and any other intelligent creatures on other planets) have only a feeble imitation of God's great intelligence. But this is still significant. We're much more like God than are other creatures (like planets, rocks, and trees), for we have intelligence and free will. We're very special in the universe, for we're like God.

In the Judeo-Christian tradition, our being made in God's *image and likeness* has great ethical significance (§1.3). It supports an ethical universalism where *all* of us (not just members of one group, race, or creed) are to be treated with dignity and respect, as we ourselves want to be treated. We're all brothers and sisters, and we have one Father, who made us in his image and likeness.

(Q4) Do kalam and fine-tuning fit well with the natural law approach sketched in Chapters 4–6?

Very well. Natural law claims that God cares for his world through laws of different sorts, including physical laws. By fine-tuning, God cares for us even through the physical constants, which make possible intelligent creatures like us.

Rationality natural-law (Chapter 4) presented the supreme practical-reason principle (about being vividly aware of the facts, avoiding falsehoods, and being consistent) and its golden-rule corollary. It's only a short jump to assume that the God of kalam and fine-tuning is supremely rational and so would know and follow these. But then he can be expected to be supremely *wise and loving*, to know all moral truths, to live consistently with these, and thus to be supremely *good*.

Biology (Chapter 5) discussed how facts about human nature (including evolutionary facts) influence our duties. And now we can see how a central aspect of God's creation – its intricate system of physical laws – makes possible the evolution of intelligent beings like us with our characteristics.

Spirituality (Chapter 6) presented the basic spirituality principle (about loving God *if he exists*). Kalam and fine-tuning give some evidence for the if-part.

(Q5) What do kalam and fine-tuning show about divine revelation?

I don't think they lead to firm results about this, but they do permit further speculation or faith. Francis Collins (2006) and Antony Flew (2007) were prominent atheists who came to God through fine-tuning; after that, they went in different directions – Collins accepting revelation (and becoming a firm Christian) but Flew hesitating to take this next step. But kalam and fine-tuning at least raise the issue.

I'd roughly follow Aquinas here. Once we believe in a personal God, we should think it likely that he'd reveal himself to us in more intimate terms. So we'd look for revelation and signs of its authenticity. Aquinas found revelation in Christianity and signs of its authenticity in Jesus's miracles. My view would be more complicated, since I think God can reveal himself through various religious traditions. I see *miracle reports* as weak evidence, since they're so common; and Jesus reportedly preferred that people believe from his words instead of his miracles (John 4:41, 4:48). I'd put more weight on the miracle of Jesus's resurrection, which was attested to by many alleged firsthand witnesses who were prepared to die for their belief. Several authors make an impressive case on these grounds for the special role of Jesus as the great mediator between God and humans.

(Q6) What do kalam and fine-tuning further reveal about divine attributes?

While kalam and fine-tuning give a vague idea of God, we can appeal to further speculation or revelation about divine attributes. Again, I'd roughly follow Aquinas. After arriving at God as *first mover* or *uncaused cause*, he used plausible arguments to stretch this to a fuller notion of God.

Regarding divine attributes, I'd like to give plausible arguments (but not here) that there's a single supreme being who created (kalam) and designed (fine-tuning) the world and who exists in an eternal and uncaused manner. This being is supremely knowing, powerful, and good; his greatness exceeds our grasp. He loves us and destines us to eternal happiness; but first we have a long meaningful journey of struggle and growth. He revealed himself to humanity both through how he created us (with reason and instinctive religiosity) and through prophets and historical religions (and in a special way through Jesus). He's wise and loving, and his supreme wisdom and love somehow provide a basis for our duties (Chapters 3 and 4–6). And finally, morality, even though it can be given a rational secular basis, is brought to a higher level when it and our lives are filled with a deep love of God.

Bibliography

Adams, Robert (1973) "A modified divine command theory of ethical wrongness," in Outka 1973, 318–47.

_____ (1979a) "Divine command metaethics modified again," *Journal of Religious Ethics* 7: 66–79 (also in Helm 1981).

_____ (1979b) "Autonomy and theological ethics," *Religious Studies* 15: 191–94.

_____ (1999) *Finite and Infinite Goods*, New York: Oxford University Press.

Al-Attar, Mariam (2010) *Islamic Ethics: Divine Command Theory in Arabo-Islamic Thought*, New York: Routledge.

Alston, William (2002) "What Euthyphro should have said," in *Philosophy of Religion: A Reader and Guide*, ed. William Craig, New Brunswick, NJ: Rutgers University Press, 283–98.

Anscombe, G. E. M. (1958) "Modern moral philosophy," *Philosophy* 33: 1–19.

Aquinas, Thomas (1274) *Summa Theologica*, 3 vols., trans. Fathers of the English Dominican Province, New York: Benziger Brothers, 1948; the natural law treatise is I–II, qq. 90–97. http://www.newadvent.org/summa.

Aronson, Eliot (1969) "The theory of cognitive dissonance," in *Advances in Experimental Social Psychology*, ed. Leonard Berkowitz, vol. 4, London: Academic Press, 1–34.

Augustine (400) "God's providence," in Swindal 2005: 107–11.

Ayer, A. J. (1946) *Language, Truth and Logic*, New York: Dover, 1952.

_____ (1988) "What I saw when I was dead," *Sunday Telegraph* (London), August 28. http://www.philosopher.eu/others-writings/a-j-ayer-what-i-saw-when-i-was-dead.

Baggett, David, and Jerry Walls (2011) *Good God: The Theistic Foundations of Morality*, New York: Oxford University Press.

Baltimore Catechism (1941) *A Catechism of Christian Doctrine*, rev. ed., no. 2 (for grades 6–8), Paterson, N.J.: St. Anthony Guild Press, 1954. http://www.catholicity.com/baltimore-catechism.

Bourget, David, and David Chalmers (2014) "What do philosophers believe?" *Philosophical Studies* 170: 465–500.

Boyd, Richard (1988) "How to be a moral realist," in *Essays on Moral Realism*, ed. Geoffrey Sayre-McCord, Ithaca, NY: Cornell University Press, 181–228.

Brickman, Philip, Don Coates, and Ronnie Janoff-Bulman (1978) "Lottery winners and accident victims: Is happiness relative?" *Journal of Personality and Social Psychology* 36: 917–27.

Brody, Baruch (1974) "Morality and religion reconsidered," in Helm 1981, 141–53.

Carson, Thomas (2000) *Value and the Good Life*, Notre Dame, IN: Notre Dame University Press.

———— (2007) "Axiology, realism, and the problem of evil," *Philosophy and Phenomenological Research* 75: 349–68.

———— (2010) *Lying and Deception*, Oxford: Oxford University Press, chapters 6–10.

———— (2012) "Divine will/divine command moral theories and the problem of arbitrariness," *Religious Studies* 48: 445–68.

Carter, Brandon (1973) "Large number coincidences and the anthropic principle in cosmology," in *Confrontation of Cosmological Theories with Observational Data* (Symposium in Krakow, Poland), Dordrecht: D. Reidel, 1974, 291–98. http://adsabs.harvard.edu/abs/1974IAUS..63..291C.

Clancy, Tim (2012) "Engineering immortality: Radical life extension and its critics," *Proceedings of the Jesuit Philosophical Association* (2012): 17–32.

Collins, Francis (2006) *The Language of God*, New York: Free Press.

Collins, Robin (1999) "A scientific argument for the existence of God: The fine-tuning design argument," in *Reason for the Hope Within*, ed. Michael Murray, Grand Rapids, MI: William B. Erdmans, 47–75.

Copan, Paul (2008) "Is Yahweh a moral monster?" *Philosophia Christi* 10: 7–37. http://www.epsociety.org/library/printable/45.pdf.

———— (2011) *Is God a Moral Monster? Making Sense of the Old Testament God*, Grand Rapids, MI: BakerBooks.

Copleston, Frederick, and Bertrand Russell (1948) "Radio debate on the existence of God." In Swindal 2005, 390–99. For some of the audio, see https://www.youtube.com/watch?v=hXPdpEJk78E#t=89.

Coulter, Chan (1989) "Moral autonomy and divine commands," *Religious Studies* 25: 117–29.

Craig, William (1994) *Reasonable Faith*, rev. ed., Wheaton, IL: Crossway.

Darwin, Charles (1871) *The Descent of Man*, 2 vols., London: John Murray.

Dawkins, Richard (1995) *River Out of Eden: A Darwinian View of Life*, New York: Basic Books.

———— (2006) *The God Delusion*, Great Britain: London.

Douglass, Frederick (1855) *My Bondage and My Freedom*, New York: Miller, Orton, and Mulligan.

du Roy, Oliver (2008) "The golden rule as the law of nature, from Origen to Martin Luther," in Neusner and Chilton 2008, 88–98.

———— (2009) *La règle d'or: Le retour d'une maxime oubliée*, Paris: Cerf.

Epstein, Greg (2009) *Good without God: What a Billion Nonreligious People Do Believe*, New York: William Morrow.

Evans, Stephen (2013) *God and Moral Obligation*, New York: Oxford University Press.

Festinger, Leon (1957) *A Theory of Cognitive Dissonance*, Stanford, CA: Stanford University Press.

Finnis, John (1997) "The good of marriage and the morality of sexual relations," *American Journal of Jurisprudence* 42: 97–134. Search for "finnismarriage.pdf" for an online version.

_____ (2011) *Natural Law and Natural Rights*, 2nd ed., New York: Oxford University Press.

Flew, Antony (1955) "Theology and falsification," in *New Essays in Philosophical Theology*, ed. Flew and Macintyre, New York: Macmillan, 96–99.

_____ (2007) *There Is a God*, New York: HarperCollins.

Frankena, William (1973a) *Ethics*, 2nd ed., Englewood Cliffs, NJ: PrenticeHall.

_____ (1973b) "Is morality logically dependent on religion?" in Outka 1973, 295–317 (also in Helm 1981).

Freud, Sigmund (1927) *The Future of an Illusion*, Garden City, NJ: Doubleday, 1957.

Fulwiler, Jennifer (2014) *Something Other Than God*, San Francisco: Ignatius Press.

Gensler, Harry (1986) "A Kantian argument against abortion," *Philosophical Studies* 49: 83–98.

_____ (1996) *Formal Ethics*, New York: Routledge.

_____ (1999) "Peter Singer – Moral hero or Nazi?" (Review of *Singer and His Critics*, edited by Dale Jamieson, and *Ethics into Action: Henry Spira and the Animal Rights Movement*, by Peter Singer), *London Times Higher Education Supplement* (Oct. 8, 1999): 26.

_____ (2009) "Darwin, ethics, and evolution," in *Darwin and Catholicism*, ed. L. Caruana, London: T&T Clark, 121–33.

_____ (2010) *Introduction to Logic*, 2nd ed., New York: Routledge, 290–335.

_____ (2011a) *Ethics: A Contemporary Introduction*, 2nd ed., New York: Routledge.

_____ (2011b) "Faith, reason, and alternatives to Genesis 1:1," *Proceedings of the Jesuit Philosophical Association* 29–47, online (search for article title).

_____ (2013) *Ethics and the Golden Rule*, New York: Routledge.

_____ (2014) *The Golden Rule*, Rockville, MD: Now You Know Media. Twelve audio/video talks, https://www.nowyouknowmedia.com/the-golden-rule-a-moral-ideal-for-the-world.html.

Gensler, Harry, and Earl Spurgin (2008) *Historical Dictionary of Ethics*, Lanham, MD: Scarecrow.

Gensler, Harry, Earl Spurgin, and James Swindal (eds.) (2004) *Ethics: Contemporary Readings*, New York: Routledge.

Glynn, Patrick (1997) *God: The Evidence*, Rocklin, CA: Prima.

Gooch, Paul (1983) "Authority and justification in theological ethics: A study in I Corinthians 7," *Journal of Religious Ethics* 11: 62–74.

Gould, Stephen (1997) "Nonoverlapping Magisteria," *Natural History* 106: 16–22.

Green, Ronald (1982) "Abraham, Isaac, and the Jewish tradition: An ethical reappraisal," *Journal of Religious Ethics* 10: 1–21.

Grimm Brothers (1812) "The old man and his grandson," http://www.gutenberg .org/ebooks/2591.

Grisez, Germain (2011) "Health care technology and justice," in *Bioethics with Liberty and Justice*, ed. Christopher Tollefsen, New York: Springer, 221–39.

Haldane, John (1989) "Voluntarism and realism in medieval ethics," *Journal of Medical Ethics* 15: 39–44.

Hare, John (2001) *God's Call: Moral Realism, God's Commands, and Human Autonomy*, Grand Rapids, MI: W. B. Eerdmans.

——— (2006) *God and Morality: A Philosophical History*, Oxford: Blackwell.

Hare, R. M. (1963) *Freedom and Reason*, Oxford: Clarendon.

Harman, Gilbert (1977) *The Nature of Morality*, New York: Oxford University Press.

Harris, Michael (2003) *Divine Command Ethics: Jewish and Christian Perspectives*, New York: RoutledgeCurzon.

Haught, John (2008) *God and the New Atheism*, Louisville, KY: Westminster John Knox.

Hawking, Stephen (1998) *A Brief History of Time*, 2nd ed., New York: Bantam Books.

Helm, Paul (ed.) (1981) *Divine Commands and Morality*, New York: Oxford University Press.

Hick, John (1978) *Evil and the God of Love*, 2nd ed., New York: Harper and Row.

Hobbes, Thomas (1651) *Leviathan*, Cambridge: Cambridge University Press, 1904.

Hume, David (1735) *A Treatise of Human Nature*, ed. L. A. Silby-Bigge, Oxford: Clarendon, 1888.

——— (1779) *Dialogues Concerning Natural Religion*, ed. Norman Kemp Smith, Indianapolis, IN: Bobbs-Merrill, 1947.

Huxley, Thomas (1866) *Selected Essays and Addresses of Thomas Henry Huxley*, ed. Philo Buck, New York: Macmillan, 1910.

Iannaccone, Lawrence (1998) "Introduction to the economics of religion," *Journal of Economic Literature* 36: 1465–95.

Idziak, Janine (ed.) (1979) *Divine Command Morality: Historical and Contemporary Readings*, New York: Edwin Mellen.

James, William (1896) *The Will to Believe*, New York: Longmans, Green, http:// www.gutenberg.org/files/26659.

Jordan, Matthew (2012) "Divine attitudes, divine commands, and the modal status of moral truths," *Religious Studies* 48: 45–60.

——— (2013a) "Theism, naturalism, and meta-ethics," *Philosophy Compass* 8: 373–80.

——— (2013b) "Divine commands or divine attitudes?" *Faith and Philosophy* 30: 159–70.

Joyce, Richard (2006) *The Evolution of Morality*, Cambridge, MA: MIT Press.

Kant, Immanuel (1781) *Critique of Pure Reason*, trans. Normal Kemp Smith, New York: St. Martin's Press.

———— (1785) *Groundwork of the Metaphysics of Morals*, trans. Herbert J. Paton, New York: Harper and Row, 1964.

———— (1788) *Critique of Practical Reason*, trans. Lewis White Beck, New York: Bobbs-Merrill.

Kaye, Sharon, and Harry Gensler (2003) "Is God the source of morality?" in *God Matters*, ed. Martin and Bernard, New York: Longman, 481–87.

Kinnier, Richard, Jerry Kernes, and Therese Dautheribes (2000) "A short list of universal moral values," *Counseling and Values* 45: 4–16.

Kripke, Saul (1972) *Naming and Necessity*, Cambridge, MA: Harvard University Press.

Küng, Hans (1993) *Global Responsibility: In Search of a New World Ethic*, New York: Continuum.

Lewis, C. S. (1952) *Mere Christianity*, New York: HarperCollins, 2001.

Loyola, Ignatius (1524) *The Spiritual Exercises*, http://www.ccel.org/ccel/ignatius/exercises.html.

MacIntyre, Alasdair (2009) *God, Philosophy, Universities*, Lanham, MD: Rowman and Littlefield.

Mackie, J. L. (1955) "Evil and Omnipotence," *Mind* 64: 200–12.

———— (1977) *Ethics: Inventing Right and Wrong*, London: Penguin.

———— (1982) *The Miracle of Theism*, New York: Oxford University Press.

Madigan, Arthur (2005) "Catholic philosophers in the U.S.," in Swindal 2005, 555–77.

Manson, Neil (ed.) (2003) *God and Design*, New York: Routledge.

Martin, James (2010) *The Jesuit Guide to (Almost) Everything*, New York: HarperOne.

Mavrodes, George (1986) "Religion and the queerness of morality," in *Rationality, Religious Belief, and Moral Commitment*, ed. Robert Audi and William Wainwright, Ithaca, NY: Cornell University Press, 213–26.

McGowan, Dale (2013) *Atheism for Dummies*, Mississauga, ON: John Wiley.

Michel, Thomas (2010) *A Christian View of Islam*, ed. Irfan Omar, Maryknoll, NY: Orbis.

Monroe, Kristen, Michael Barton, and Ute Klingemann (1990) "Altruism and the theory of rational action: Rescuers of Jews in Nazi Europe," *Ethics* 101: 103–22.

Moore, G. E. (1903) *Principia Ethica*, Cambridge: Cambridge University Press.

Moser, Paul (2008) *The Elusive God*, New York: Cambridge University Press.

Moser, Paul, and Paul Copan (2003) *The Rationality of Theism*, New York: Routledge.

Murphy, Mark (2011) "The Natural Law tradition in ethics," *Stanford Encyclopedia of Philosophy* (Winter 2011), ed. Edward N. Zalta, http://plato.stanford.edu/archives/win2011/entries/natural-law-ethics.

Newman, John (1870) *An Essay in Aid of a Grammar of Assent*, New York: Catholic Publication Society.

Nielsen, Kai (1961) "Some remarks on the independence of morality from religion," *Mind* 70: 175–86.

———— (1990) *Ethics without God*, Amherst, NY: Prometheus.

Outka, Gene, and John P. Reeder (eds.) (1973) *Religion and Morality: A Collection of Essays*, Garden City, NY: Anchor.

Pennington, Kenneth (2008) "Lex naturalis and ius natural," *Jurist* 68: 569–91.

Plantinga, Alvin (1974) *God, Freedom, and Evil*. New York: Harper and Row.

———— (1983) "Advice to Christian philosophers," in Swindal 2005, 478–87.

———— (2006) "Evolution and design," in *For Faith and Clarity*, ed. James Beilby, Grand Rapids, MI: Baker Academic, 201–18.

———— (2011) *Where the Conflict Really Lies: Science, Religion, and Naturalism*, New York: Oxford University Press.

Pope Francis (2013) "Morning Meditation for 22 May 2013," http://w2.vatican .va/content/francesco/en/cotidie/2013/documents/papa-francesco-cotidie_ 20130522_to-do-good.html.

———— (2015) *Laudato Si'* (letter on ecology), http://w2.vatican.va/content/ francesco/en/encyclicals/documents /papa-francesco_20150524_enciclica- laudato-si.html.

Putnam, Hilary (1973) "Meaning and reference," *Journal of Philosophy* 70: 699– 711.

Quine, Willard (1986) *Philosophy of Logic*, 2nd ed., Cambridge, MA: Harvard University Press.

Quinn, Philip (1978) *Divine Commands and Moral Requirements*, New York: Oxford University Press.

Rees, D. A. (1956–57) "The ethics of divine commands," *Proceedings of the Aristotelian Society* 57: 83–106.

Reiner, Hans (1983) "The golden rule and the natural law," in *Duty and Inclination*, trans. M. Santos, The Hague: Martinus Nijhoff, 271–93.

Ritchie, Angus (2012) *From Morality to Metaphysics: The Theistic Implications of our Ethical Commitments*, New York: Oxford University Press.

Romig, Robert (1984) *Reasonable Religion*, Buffalo, NY: Prometheus.

Ross, W. D. (1930) *The Right and the Good*, Oxford: Clarendon Press.

Ruse, Michael (1986) *Taking Darwin Seriously*, Oxford: Basil Blackwell.

Russell, Bertrand (1905) "On Denoting," *Mind* 15: 479–93.

———— (1957) *Why I Am Not a Christian*, ed. Paul Edwards, New York: Simon and Schuster. Many of these essays are also online; see http://www.skeptic.ca/ bertrand_russell_reading_list.htm.

Saeed, Sohaib (2010) "The golden rule: An Islamic-dialogic perspective," paper at Edinburgh Festival of Spirituality of Peace, http://dialogicws.files.wordpress .com/2010/07/goldenrule_saeed1.pdf.

Shapiro, Rami (2015) *The Golden Rule and Games People Play*, Woodstock, VT: Jewish Lights.

Sheiman, Bruce (2009) *An Atheist Defends Religion*, New York: Penguin.

Smith, Quinton (2001) "The Metaphilosophy of Naturalism," *Philo* 4: 195–215, http://holtz.org/Library/Philosophy.

Sober, Elliott (2009) "Absence of evidence and evidence of absence," *Philosophical Studies* 143 (2009): 63–90.

Spitzer, Robert (2010) *New Proofs for the Existence of God*, Grand Rapids, MI: W.B. Eerdmans.

Suárez, Francisco (1612) "On laws and God the lawgiver," in Idziak 1979, 73–91.

Swinburne, Richard (2004) *The Existence of God*, 2nd ed., New York: Oxford University Press.

Swindal, James, and Harry Gensler (eds.) (2005) *The Sheed and Ward Anthology of Catholic Philosophy*, Lanham, MD: Rowman and Littlefield.

Tait, Katharine (1975) *My Father, Bertrand Russell*, New York: Harcourt, Brace, Jovanovich.

Telushkin, Joseph (2006–9) *A Code of Jewish Ethics*, 2 vols., New York: Bell Tower, 1:10–2, 2:9–15.

Troll, Christian (2008) "Future Christian-Muslim engagement," paper at a Cambridge meeting between Christians and Muslims, http://chiesa.espresso .repubblica.it/articolo/208895?eng=y.

Turnbull, Colin (1972) *The Mountain People*, New York: Simon and Schuster.

Vatican (2009) *In Search of a Universal Ethic: A New Look at the Natural Law*, a report of the Vatican International Theological Commission, http://www.vatican.va/roman_curia/congregations/cfaith/cti_documents/ rc_con_cfaith_doc_20090520_legge-naturale_en.html.

Vatican II (1962–65) http://www.vatican.va/archive/hist_councils/ii_vatican_ council/index.htm.

Wainwright, William (2005) *Religion and Morality*, Burlington, VT: Ashgate.

Wattles, Jeffrey (1996) *The Golden Rule*, New York: Oxford University Press.

Williams, Bernard (1972) "God, morality, and prudence," in Helm 1981, 135–40.

Wine, Sherwin (1985) *Judaism beyond God*, Farmington Hills, MI: Society for Humanistic Humanism.

Zagzebski, Linda (2004) *Divine Motivation Theory*, New York: Cambridge University Press.

Index